A Rehabber's Tale

A Rehabber's Tale

The Reality of Fixing and Flipping Real Estate

Richard J. Warren

iUniverse, Inc.
New York Lincoln Shanghai

A Rehabber's Tale
The Reality of Fixing and Flipping Real Estate

iUniverse books may be ordered through booksellers or by contacting:

iUniverse
2021 Pine Lake Road, Suite 100
Lincoln, NE 68512
www.iuniverse.com
1-800-Authors (1-800-288-4677)

Because of the dynamic nature of the Internet, any Web addresses
or links contained in this book may have changed
since publication and may no longer be valid.

The information, ideas, and suggestions in this book are not intended
to render professional advice. Before following any suggestions
contained in this book, you should consult your personal accountant
or other financial advisor. Neither the author nor the publisher shall
be liable or responsible for any loss or damage allegedly arising as
a consequence of your use or application of any information or
suggestions in this book.

ISBN: 978-0-595-48631-1

Printed in the United States of America

This book is dedicated to Frank Warren, my dad;
he left this world way too soon.

Destiny is not a matter of chance; it is a matter of choice. It is not a thing to be waited for; it is a thing to be achieved! —William Jennings Bryan

Contents

Acknowledgments

I don't think that anyone can truly understand what is involved in writing a book unless they have done it. Without a doubt, it is one of the most difficult tasks that I have ever attempted; I now have a totally different perspective when I enter a bookstore. I have a new-found respect for all of those authors whose books are on the shelves, I feel their pain!

I clearly recall hearing my father talk about the book he was going to write. He was well educated and certainly had the ability to do it, but life always seemed to get in the way. He was an accountant by profession and much of his focus was on the coming of "tax season." The preparation of tax returns was a blessing and a curse. It brought in much needed money, but also consumed valuable time. I recall many childhood conversations about all of the magical things that would happen "after tax season." Unfortunately, they never seemed to occur. There was always something else that needed to be done. Sadly, the book was never written when he passed away at the age of 56. I did not want to have the book that was in me go unwritten.

In so many areas I am the consummate do-it-yourselfer, but this is not a project that I could have done alone. There were so many people who helped me along the way. I know how an Academy Award winner must feel, having so many people to thank before they are ushered off the stage. There is always the fear of not thanking someone who truly deserves it.

First and foremost, I need to thank my brother, Ed Sellner. After serving in Vietnam as a Marine, he came home and started a small construction company. He essentially worked by himself at first, doing roofing, siding and whatever else came along. I was a ten-year-old kid when he hired me to help him. I clearly recall my first assignment; I was to hold up the end of a gutter while he nailed it in place. I went on to help him whenever he needed that extra pair of hands. As I got older I worked with him during the summer, and my responsibilities grew as I did. I learned so much from working with him. But he taught me so much more than how to swing a hammer, he taught me about life. Through him I saw the ups and downs that people experienced and learned how to cope with them. I learned the value of hard work, and I have rarely come across anyone who worked harder than he did. I can't imagine where I would be today if he hadn't taken me under his wing and had the patience to let me learn from my mistakes.

This book never would have happened without Michelle Caldwell, of Caldwell Consulting. She is my success coach, mentor, and friend. She kept me on-track and guided me along as I sailed through uncharted waters. In a project like this it is very easy to lose focus and put things off. Her support and input were invaluable and I can't thank her enough. She is fond of saying, "It's not what you know; it's what you do with what you know." She has helped me to achieve more than I ever could have imagined.

My friend and fellow rehabber, Tamara Bostrom, was a tremendous asset to me by providing her own insight. She is a truly amazing woman who is not only a rehabber, but also a writer and professional poker player. Not only did she contribute by providing a tale for the book, but her assistance in proofreading and editing the manuscript was priceless. Tamara and I also share the same birthday, April 12, but, as she is fond of reminding me, she is two decades younger. I am so thankful for her advice and input, but I am also thankful that I have never had to sit opposite her at a poker table!

Another individual, who has been a tremendous asset to me both personally and in business, is Sean Brown. I met Sean several years ago at a networking group. He had been a 747 pilot for a major airline, but turned to real estate after the turmoil in the airline industry following 9/11. He was specializing in Las Vegas investment real estate when he came to the realization that the rate of growth being experienced was unsustainable. He looked for other areas to invest in on behalf of his clients, but soon found that that was no easy task. This led him to create the National Association of Residential Real Estate Investment Advisors (NARREIA). NARREIA's mission is to seek out investment opportunities in markets all across the country using a group of carefully screened advisors. It was through Sean and NARREIA that I came to find some of my most profitable markets. Sean also provided the foreword for this book and I can't possibly thank him enough.

I owe a great deal to Darci Poloni, of Poloni & Associates, both for providing a tale as well as for her advice, support, and encouragement. As my personal attorney, she has been a tremendous help to my family and me. It seems she is on a mission to single-handedly give attorneys a good name.

Anyone who invests in real estate knows that real estate and taxes go hand in hand. What a treasure it is to have an accountant who is not only a consummate professional, but also a real estate investor herself. Judy Cruden, of Judith Cruden, CPA, is a wealth of information when it comes to the tax ramifications of investing in real estate. The tale she contributed is a powerful example of why it is so important to do your homework ahead of time. While I thank her, I think many readers will thank her as well.

So many rehabbers contributed their own stories to this book. By their choice, some are mentioned by first name only. One such rehabber is Cindy from Connecticut. Working in the corporate world, she harbored the rehabber's fantasy for twenty years before trying her hand. We also have Tony and Danny, two young guys with big dreams. I fully expect that all of them will meet with great success.

Frank Adams, otherwise known as "all-cash," provided great insight into rehabbing on a budget. His common sense approach is refreshing to say the least. He also has an exit strategy that has lead him to a point that he calls "financial critical mass." I truly appreciate his contribution.

Minna Javanainen is another amazing woman. She tired of working in the corporate world and gave up a well paying position to pursue her passion. It didn't come easy for her and she met a lot of roadblocks along the way. But, like that battery-powered bunny on television, she just kept going. Her results were fantastic and she is an inspiration for anyone looking to venture out on their own.

Connie Brzowski, from Texas, turned to rehabbing as a way to get better deals on investment property. She soon found that she had a knack for it. She has a great sense of humor and is eager to share what she has learned. In addition to providing a tale, Connie has her own real estate blog and is a regular contributor to real estate Web sites. I was ecstatic when she agreed to contribute.

Last, but by no means least, I have to thank my wife, Kathi. She has come to love rehabbing as much as I do. By her own admission, a neat freak, she has come to appreciate the fact that when you are looking for rehab candidates, "icky" is good. She also has a knack for finding properties and has been the one that located many of our deals. In addition, she has the vision to see what a house could be instead of what it is. More importantly, she puts up with me while I do my "stuff." Writing a book takes a lot of time and energy, and I thank her for being patient with me.

If I have forgotten any one, you have my apology as well as my sincere thanks.

Richard Warren
www.RehabersEye.com

Foreword

Rehabbing houses is a fun and easy way to make a lot of money on your way to early retirement. After all, if you watch those house flipping shows on television, you can see that if you buy a house for $100,000 and sell it for $200,000, you can make $100,000 on the deal.

Only they forgot to tell you about the closing costs, both when you buy it and when you sell it. Nor did they mention any commissions if you choose to use a real estate agent. Oh, and the costs to hold the property for the month or six that it takes to fix and sell it weren't calculated in there, either. The overruns, the redos, the unplanned repairs ... none of that ever seems to be factored into the bottom line. Wouldn't it be nice if someone could explain all that before you get into the business?

For many people, 2003 to 2005 will be remembered as one of the most insane real estate markets this country has ever experienced. *Monthly* appreciation of 3–10% caused some housing markets to double in price during that period. Watching this appreciation, my colleagues and I knew that it could not continue for long. We recognized that our clients needed to invest in other markets in order to diversify their real estate portfolios. This drove us to found NARREIA, the National Association of Residential Real Estate Investment Advisors. It is our mission to alert real estate investors to the myriad opportunities that are out there. Most real estate investors end up investing in their local market because it's the only place they know about. Very few have the time, resources, or drive to educate themselves about other markets nationwide and use that information to find the best investment opportunities. We started our organization to help investors separate the wheat from the chaff, introduce them to the best markets and connect them with agents, builders, and developers who could help them acquire properties across the country. This also allowed our clients to diversify their portfolios geographically in the event of a downturn in one of the markets they had chosen.

It was early in the boom when I met Rich Warren. An unassuming, friendly, and genuinely likeable guy, Rich had joined a local networking group that some colleagues and I had recently started. With Rich's help and unfailing participation, we grew it into one of the most successful networking groups in Las Vegas.

At one particular networking meeting, we were explaining how we learned that Ely, Nevada (pronounced ee-lee) was subject to quite a few economic issues that were causing this tiny little mining town to be primed for a local boom. An old copper mine had been purchased and restarted by one of the largest mining companies in the world. A new power plant was going to be built less than an hour north of the town, and there was rumor of yet another prison being built in the area. One of the largest natural gas fields had been discovered on the border of Utah and Nevada, and Ely is one of the closest towns on the Nevada side. With a population of only 8,500 and the prospect of several thousand jobs being added to the area, it was pretty clear that there was going to be a housing shortage. Local property managers already had a waiting list of tenants looking for houses to rent.

This got Rich thinking. There was almost no building going on in Ely and the average house in the area was over 70 years old. Even if you wanted to buy a rental property, you'd be purchasing a building that was in need of serious work. But that was okay with Rich. He had done an extensive rehab on the East Coast before he moved out to Las Vegas. He possessed the very valuable experience of having actually completed a project before deciding to get involved with the opportunities in Ely.

So Rich, his wife Kathi, and I went up to the mining town to do a little prospecting and Rich struck gold. He was enamored with the mountainous views and historic feel that White Pine County had to offer. Where many real estate investors would turn and flee from a property, Rich's eyes would literally light up at the potential. While I have taken advantage of a broad range of real estate investments over the years, I grew up as a small town handyman's son and consider myself a rehabber at heart. And yet some of the deals that Rich was considering were deals that I would not have gotten involved with. This is why Rich is tripling and quadrupling (and more) in Ely and the rest of us are not. It takes vision, heart, and a lot of hard work to do what he's doing. But if you have those and are willing to put in the effort, you, too, can do what Rich is doing.

Before the boom, one of the few television shows that featured real estate anything was "*This Old House.*" But that show was more about remodeling your cottage in New England than it was about making money. The channels wanted to capitalize on the out-of-control buzz about real estate investing, but your typical real estate transaction is about as fun and exciting as attending a convention for tax preparers. What they needed was an investment vehicle that had drama, risk, and reward and could be wrapped up in a 22-minute program.

So the house flipping television show genre was born. There's drama. There's risk. There's reward. And according to most of the shows, there was A LOT of reward. They could control the suspense by making it seem like deadlines were brick walls or by showing a conflict with a contractor, but they knew they needed to show that the flippers were making money. Think about it, could the series continue past a few shows if the flippers continually lost money? The series were much more sustainable if the outcome was regularly favorable and they were more infectious if the "profits" were large.

This lead to inflated results on the shows. They would subtract the purchase price of the property from the projected or actual sales price of the property and then take out the cost of the repairs. They would then present this number as some type of profit; although some shows were craftier with their wording as to not imply that the number was profit but left room for the unlearned to incorrectly infer it as so.

The result was a large wave of first time real estate investors who wanted to become rehabbers. For many, not only would the flip be the first rehab project they had ever done, but it would be the first real estate investment transaction that they had ever gone through. Real estate investing is challenging enough the first few times, but adding the stress and capital risk required when you have little or no real estate investment experience is not necessarily the best way to approach it.

And that is why this book is so valuable to anyone looking to rehab a property. This is especially true if you are preparing to do one of your first rehabs. The reality of rehabbing is far from the fantasy that many have come to envision. But there is much in Rich's book that will benefit the experienced investor as well: tips from other rehabbers, advice on how to anticipate and prepare for changing market conditions, and true to life accounts of good jobs gone bad.

You can learn a lot from Rich's experience and from the stories included in his book. Rich will strip off the silky soft veil that the house flipping television shows have draped over rehabbing. He will expose the dirty underbelly of the process and show that rehabbing is not just about replacing a little carpet and paint, that it is more about ripping out kitchens and bathrooms, tearing off roofs, and redoing plumbing and electrical wiring. It's also about buying right, because that is where you really make your money.

Rehabbing is hard work. Rehabbing is dirty work. Rehabbing is risky work. Rehabbing is not as glamorous as flipping a high rise luxury unit. Rehabbing is real investing. But rehabbing, done right, is extremely rewarding. It can provide a return on your investment that is hard to match by any other real estate investment vehicle except under the most fantastic market conditions.

Sean Brown
NARREIA
The National Association of Residential Real Estate Investment Advisors
www.NARREIA.com

Introduction

The future belongs to those who see possibilities before they become obvious.—John Scully, former CEO of Pepsi & Apple Computer

These days it seems like everyone thinks that they can find their fortune in real estate. We all know someone who bought a house many years ago that is now worth a tremendous amount of money. Unfortunately many people have a need for immediate gratification and are not willing to work in order to create this fortune. They ignore the fact that the people to which they are referring to purchased their home twenty, thirty or even forty years ago and worked hard to pay off their mortgage. That coupled with the natural appreciation over many years makes it appear that they created this wealth from nothing.

The house they purchased in 1955 for $10,000 may be worth almost half a million dollars today. On paper that looks like a phenomenal gain, in actuality it doesn't even represent a double-digit yearly return. These can be attributed more to the effects of time than any real investment savvy. The dollar that George Washington is alleged to have thrown across the Delaware River would be worth over 3.6 billion dollars today if it had been invested at 10%!

While real estate is one of the safest investments that you can make, it should not be treated as a get-rich-quick scheme. The economy of the United States is one that is subject to cycles of boom and bust. When it is booming it appears that the good times will never end. When it is in a bust cycle it seems that the bad times are here forever. The truth is that we will always have these fluctuations. Every boom seems to have a different leader whether it is gold, oil, junk bonds, technology stocks or real estate. When we look back at a cycle after it has ended it seems that we should have seen the end coming.

Just before the 1929 stock market crash blue-collar people were buying stocks on margin (borrowing money to buy). When gold peaked at over $800 per ounce in 1980, people were lining up to buy when they should have been looking to sell. The oil boom of the 1970s led to many bank failures since loans were made based on rising oil prices. The subsequent collapse of prices in the oil markets caused many people holding these loans to default and foreclosures to rise in the oil states. Junk bonds were all the rage at one time only to come crashing down with prominent junk bond traders disgraced and jailed. The dot-com companies were the hottest things in the "new economy." They became the dot-gone companies when people realized that even tech companies still needed to turn a profit.

Now it seems to be real estate's turn. The appreciation of real estate in most parts of the country created a new wave of investors. All you had to do was buy anything and it would go up. These novice investors thought of themselves as experts because they had made money. But just like a game of musical chairs, the music eventually stopped and many people were facing financial ruin. These "wanna-be" real estate tycoons didn't do it alone; they had plenty of help.

A slew of new mortgage products came on the market. You could buy with no down payment. You could obtain adjustable rate loans with an introductory period of artificially low payments, or loans with negative amortization where the loan balance would actually grow each month. Don't have the income necessary to qualify? No problem, let's just use a no-documentation loan. It seemed that anyone could get a loan. But it didn't matter because the real estate was appreciating incredibly fast and there was no end in sight.

There were many cases of low paid workers using one of these loans to qualify for a house that they couldn't really afford. The idea was to refinance just before the interest rate was going to adjust to a higher figure. Early on in the boom this may have worked but when the appreciation stopped the borrowers found that they were stuck with the loan. The payments went up but their income didn't and the result was another foreclosure.

While the boom continued, it seemed that everywhere you went people were talking about real estate. It was time to buy and cash in on the craze. It was easy. Just refinance your house to pull out cash, and then use that cash as a down payment on an investment property. In theory that isn't necessarily a bad thing. The reality was that most of the people employing these tactics had no idea about real estate investing. The end result was that they would pay too much for an investment property that wouldn't come close to generating enough rental income to pay for the mortgage and expenses. This could result in the loss of both the rental property and the home they refinanced in order to invest.

The current meltdown in the sub-prime lending market has made it impossible for many people to refinance. Lending standards have been tightened to pre-insanity levels. You now actually need a down payment and the ability to repay the loan, imagine that!

Another effect of the boom occurred in the job market. Plenty of people saw selling real estate as a way to make easy money. They obtained their real estate license and began selling properties as a sideline. They didn't know any more than the people that they were representing. After all, how hard was it to sell a house? Just put a sign on the lawn, list it on the MLS, and collect the commission. Now that the market has cooled off, many of these newbies are leaving the business, much to the relief of the true professionals.

A phenomenon that seems to occur in every boom is the rise of self-proclaimed experts. They will teach you everything that you need to know in order to make a fortune in the latest fad. Book titles seem to scream at you, *"Buy Gold!," "Make a Fortune with Oil Futures," "Flip Your Way to Real Estate Profits,"* and the list goes on. It seems that many of these experts are just looking to cash in on the current craze without offering any truly unique insights or advice.

The real estate "guru" is no exception. Once staples of late night television, these gurus are now everywhere. There are some that have very good information to share but many others that do not. There is so much bad information being bandied about by these so-called experts, that it seems as if they are just looking to make money by telling people what they want to hear. Many books and seminars are nothing more than a sales pitch for a higher priced program.

Companies have also sprung up claiming to exist for the purpose of teaching people how to invest. They claim that they will educate you so that you can make a fortune investing in real estate. They then use "graduates" of the course to recruit new students. These new students pay thousands of dollars for this "education" with a large portion of that fee being paid as a commission to the "graduate" who recruited the new "student." These programs are more about making money through these fees than they are about education. Most of the graduates of the program never even make a real estate purchase but claim that they can help others do so. As the real estate market cools and fewer people see real estate as easy money most of these programs will die off. Unfortunately a lot of people will have been sucked in and lost a lot of money.

My inspiration for writing this book is actually an article that I read by a respected real estate agent. He was touting the virtues of rehabbing properties yet it quickly became clear that he knew very little about the subject. He was suggesting that you buy properties at a discount of 15–20%, then hire contractors to do the necessary repairs, and quickly sell the home for a tidy profit. My experience in this area quickly told me that what this agent was preaching would virtually guarantee a loss for anyone who tried to implement his recommendations.

The proliferation of television shows implying that you can flip your way to wealth suggests to people that rehabbing is easy. The show format always seems to be the same. Someone buys a home with expectations of great profits. They run into problems towards the middle of the episode but manage to come through at the end. They will have an open house and immediately sell. The show will then show what they paid, what they spent and the gross profit. What they don't show is all of the different costs involved, which may have left them with very little or no profit in the end.

In May of 2007, Fox News in Atlanta exposed "*Flip This House*" as a fraud. This program takes you through the trials and tribulations of investors as they try to renovate real estate for profit. Many of the houses that they claimed to rehab and sell were in fact still on the market. Much of the work was staged for the show and in at least one case the person being featured didn't even own the house. The A&E Television Network has claimed that they were unaware of the situation and have since replaced the host.

Many people are constantly seeking out new ways to make money. You often hear people talking about whether it is a good time or a bad time to invest in real estate. Is the market going up or down? When you are rehabbing real estate it doesn't matter how the market is doing. You are not relying on market appreciation to provide you with a profit; you make your profit by buying right. Most people who fail when rehabbing real estate do so because they paid too much for the property or seriously underestimated how much time or money would be necessary to rehab the property.

Real estate can be an outstanding investment. It offers leverage that few other investments can match. With a small down payment you can own a property with excellent appreciation potential as well as immediate cash flow. Distressed properties offer a prospect of instant equity that can't be found in other investment vehicles. But it is not without risk or hard work. My goal here is to help you manage that risk and to present you with the reality of the work involved. This will give you a much better chance for success. Real estate investing is a business not a hobby. If you treat it like a business it can reward you in ways that most businesses can't.

My earlier career was in the financial services industry where I went on to become a *Certified Financial Planner* (CFP). I clearly recall a very successful industry veteran sharing a success secret with me when I began. He said that if you spend ten years working like other people are unwilling to work, you can spend the rest of your life living like other people are unable to live. Nowhere is that more true than in real estate investing.

I have been rehabbing real estate for almost fifteen years. I have done numerous projects of my own. I have also partnered on projects and acted as a consultant on several others. I felt it was time to share the things that I have learned over the years so that others may enjoy the same successes that I have.

Are you ready to begin?

Part I

The Art of Rehab

Chapter 1

Why Rehab?

The best way to see the future is to create it.—**Unknown**

Who hasn't dreamed of making a fortune in real estate? It is a common fantasy among people of all ages. "I'll buy a run-down house, do a little fixing up and resell at a huge profit!" The TV shows make it look easy, but how realistic is it?

There is definitely a need for housing rehabilitation. There was a housing boom in this country that mirrored the baby boom. As servicemen returned home from World War II and started families, new forms of housing emerged. William Levitt started a new style of community with *Levittown*. The concept of suburbia and affordable housing was born. William Levitt's idea was to provide communities for these new families to live in filled with good basic homes that the average person could afford. Before long, similar new communities were springing up all across the country.

This post-war building boom has created an abundance of older homes today. Many of these homes are in need of anything from cosmetic updates to full-blown rehabilitation. This in turn has created a fantastic opportunity for those who wish to create wealth by investing in real estate rehabs. With opportunity, however, comes risk. Risk cannot be avoided but it can be managed. The idea is to learn as much as possible from the mistakes and triumphs of others and apply it to your own situation. So while opportunity and risk go hand-in-hand so do risk and reward.

My first rehab experience happened out of necessity. I was living in Long Island, New York at the time. I had been renting a house that was for sale, the market was slow and the house had been listed for almost two years. It was eventually sold and I was given 90 days to find a new place. I didn't have much money but I also did not want to keep on renting. Despite the slow sales pace, or perhaps because of it, the rental market was very strong and rents were pretty high. I did not want to continue to throw money away on rent when a monthly mortgage payment wouldn't be much higher.

Because I had less than $15,000 to work with I had to look at the low end of the market, which was in areas where I really didn't want to live. Mind you, we're not talking about living in a ghetto, just areas that are not as nice as I would like. These were blue-collar neighborhoods with row after row of cookie-cutter houses. As I was driving from one of these areas to another I passed through a sleepy town filled with nice older homes on tree lined streets I remember thinking to myself "now this is where I want to live." The only problem was that the smaller houses in this area were twice what I could afford to pay.

As luck would have it, just as I was about to exit the town I came across a house that caught my eye. It was a run-down home on a nice piece of property, the proverbial worst house on the block. It was vacant but there was no indication that it was for sale so I drove away. Later that afternoon, as I was looking through the real estate section of the classifieds, I saw a listing in that very town. The ad had been placed by a local real estate agent and stated that they had a bank-owned property for sale at a price that was about $20,000 higher than my maximum. I called the number in the advertisement.

While speaking to the agent, she said that this was a house that the bank had foreclosed on and they would be accepting bids. I made an appointment to meet the agent the next day to look at the property and, you guessed it, it was the same house. This house, to say the least, had some serious issues and was being sold "as-is." The yard was overgrown and had been neglected for some time. The roof needed to be replaced, the windows were in bad shape and the aluminum siding needed to be redone. The inside needed to be totally gutted. Like an idiot I was thinking, "I can do this!"

I discussed the bidding process with the agent and she suggested that I make an offer I was comfortable with. She said that she expected it would sell for less than the listed price but she couldn't coach me on what to offer because she represented the bank. Since this was the first time I had worked with an agent, I didn't realize how lucky I was to find one that was ethical. While I do believe that the vast majority of agents are ethical, an agent that is less than scrupulous can be a nightmare.

She then brought up one issue that I hadn't considered at that point … financing. Due to the condition of the house it would be impossible to get conventional financing. This is where the slow real estate market helped me, in order for the bank to unload this house they would have to be willing to finance it. They were offering an adjustable rate only with a minimum of 10% down. I didn't understand the significance at the time but they were going to have to hold this loan in their own loan portfolio and they would only hold adjustable rate loans. Because they were eager to get rid of the property they would also be a little more lenient in their underwriting.

Since the bank required 10% down plus closing costs and I only had about $15,000 that meant that the most I could bid was about $100,000. I wound up submitting a bid for $95,000 and hoped for the best. It turned out that the bank received two other bids in that same price range and would decide on which one to accept. While the bank was going over the offers, one of the other bidders withdrew their bid. The other remaining bidder had horrible credit and the bank accepted my offer. Lucky me!

The fun was just beginning. The bank assigned me to a rookie loan officer who was doing one of his first deals. He was absolutely clueless when it came to knowing what to do next. Since I knew nothing about the mortgage process, it was truly a case of the blind leading the blind. All this time the clock was ticking as my moving day approached. A deal that should have taken about 30 days was nearing the end of its second month and I had to move. I wound up staying with family members for several weeks while I waited to close escrow on the house.

Everything I owned was in boxes left at various friends' and relatives' houses.

At last, closing day arrived. I walked into the conference room at the office of the bank's attorney and was faced with half a dozen people I had never seen before. But it was ok because as I walked in everyone was glad to see me. What I didn't realize was that they were smiling because they were all there to get a piece of the pie, and I was the pie!

The closing documents started going back and forth between the title officer, the bank attorney, and my attorney. Papers were being passed to me for signature and I felt like I didn't have a clue as to what was happening. After all of this it was time for the checks. I had been instructed to bring a certified check for the closing fees. The down payment was already held in escrow. But it seems that there was a discrepancy, the check was not enough to cover all of the charges. The rookie loan officer had given me the amount, but it seems he goofed. He forgot to include the impound amount for taxes and insurance. They told me it was ok, they would accept a personal check. The only problem was that I didn't have the funds in the account to cover it. I wrote the check anyway and then had to scramble to borrow money and get it in the bank so that the check would clear. At this point they handed me the keys and everyone smiled, shook my hand and congratulated me. I was left with a sense of dread, had I done the right thing?

I was now a homeowner. After the ordeal of closing escrow, I went to my "new" home. As I walked through it looked worse than ever and I thought, "What in the world was I thinking?" My older sister had purchased a home when she first got married that I referred to as "the hovel." It was a real dump, but it was all she could afford. Since she was the one person in my family who would understand, I invited her over. As she walked through the house, I could see from her expression that she thought I had truly lost my mind. Shortly after she arrived she made some excuse and she left, I half expected her tires to burn rubber as she drove away.

That evening I spent my first night in the house. I didn't sleep much, as you can imagine. So many thoughts kept racing through my mind, I was sure that I had made a big mistake. Could I just sell it? No way, not in this market. Maybe I could just do some cosmetic repairs? Again, no way. I was stuck.

The new day brought with it a new attitude. Since I was stuck with it I would make the best of it. I started by cleaning up the mess and getting rid of the trash. I purchased a couple of large buckets of cheap white paint and gave it all a quick coat. I was going to gut every room but it at least gave it a clean fresh look for the time being. I proceeded to clean up the yard and make it a little more presentable. It wasn't much but it helped.

After I did this basic clean up it was time to get started on the real work. The first thing that I did was an overall evaluation of the house. I determined what it needed and assigned everything a priority. This became my action plan. I divided things into three categories, 1) must do, 2) should do and 3) would like to do. After putting things into their proper category, I refined things even further by giving each list its own priority order. The list was overwhelming but at least I had a better handle on what needed to be done. Since I was on a tight budget, I also divided the lists by the expected cost of each item.

Putting things down on paper had me feeling better about the project. It was a lot of work but I had time since I was living there as well. I also had the advantage of having worked with my brother in his construction company as a teen and had learned the basics of home renovation. But if this had been a property that I needed to rehab and sell in a hurry, I would have been in big trouble. I didn't have the cash for the repairs, but I did have a brand new credit card, and before long that piece of plastic was smoking.

With my list in hand I was ready to get started on my first priority, getting hot water. I thought that this would be easy since the boiler was fairly new. It was an oil-fired system so I arranged for a delivery of heating oil and asked for the Oil Company to send a service technician to tune up and start the furnace. The oil arrived on schedule and the service technician showed up a short time later. He was working on the boiler for only about ten minutes when he returned with some unexpected news, the boiler was no good. This came as a shock because it was obviously a fairly new unit. The technician explained that it had not been properly shut down. The house had been vacant and without power for over a year, this caused all of the gaskets and seals in the boiler to dry out and fail. The only solution was a new furnace. The bad news was that this meant an unexpected expense of $2500; the good news was that it could be financed. Just what I needed, another payment. What could I do? I had heat and hot water a few days later.

In a classic case of one thing leading to another, the next problem surfaced when the water to the heating system was turned on. The house was heated using a hot water baseboard system. As the water began circulating through the system, I had geysers spouting everywhere. Since the system had not been properly shut down and drained, the water in the pipes froze. The frozen water expanded and the pipes burst in multiple locations. When I realized what was happening I shut the water off and thought about what I should do next. All of this plumbing needed to be replaced and I had planned to do it room by room as I renovated. I did not want to be doing this now so I looked for another solution. I went to the local Home Depot where I was quickly becoming a regular. I talked to someone in the plumbing department who had a unique idea. He suggested that I go to an auto parts store and buy some automotive heater hose and a bunch of clamps. I took his suggestion and tried it out. I cut out the broken sections of pipe and spliced them back together with the heater hose, it worked like a charm. This is not something that I would recommend as a long-term solution, but as a short-term fix, it was perfect.

I did not have a home inspection prior to buying this house. My thinking was that the house probably needed everything and I would buy it regardless of what the report said. The house had been vacant for over a year and the power and water had been shut off. An inspector would not have been able to find these problems without water and electric anyway and I was buying the house as-is. However, I do believe in getting inspections prior to purchase whenever possible. You can always use the inspection results as a way to get additional concessions or price reductions from the seller. An inspection can also reveal problems that you were not expecting leaving you with the option of walking away from the deal.

After this crisis had past I started with the roof because that seemed to be the most pressing need. The house had water coming in everywhere when it rained. This water had caused considerable damage to the rest of the house as well. I had done quite a bit of roofing over the years and I figured this job wouldn't take more than a week. A month later I was still working on it. The moisture had attracted a colony of carpenter ants and the damage to the roof deck had been extensive. Most of the wood needed to be replaced. It was a lot more work, took a lot more time and cost a lot more than expected. Unfortunately, I came to find out that in rehab this is the rule not the exception.

When the roof was complete, it was time to move on to the next phase of the project. The timing was excellent since winter was approaching and the next part of the project would be indoors. That really didn't narrow it down much since just about everything on the inside needed to be replaced.

I decided to tackle the bedrooms first. I figured that they wouldn't be too hard or too expensive. The plan was to gut each room one at a time and hang new drywall. I had also decided to move some doorways and reconfigure some closets. This was something that I thought I should be able to do fairly quickly as well. It started out fine and there were no major surprises. I also learned something else at this point; working full-time and rehabbing a house is not easy! I found myself goofing off a lot of times when I should have been working and the project slowed down considerably. I was able to get past this period of apathy by setting a deadline with a consequence. The holidays were coming so I invited the family over for a party. Now I had a date when the living areas had to be finished and I went to work.

It was at this phase of the project that I learned another valuable lesson: just because you know how something is done, doesn't mean that you can do it well. I know how to hit a baseball, but that doesn't mean that I can hit one thrown by a major league pitcher at 95 mph! The same holds true when it comes to taping drywall. I know how it is done but one attempt at doing it convinced me that it was time to bring in some outside help. Of course that wasn't in the budget either. This is another major lesson in rehab: you need to know what you don't know. If you do not know how to do something to an acceptable standard then you need to bring in a professional. Having to call in a pro when you didn't expect to can blow your budget quickly.

I finished hanging the drywall and had someone come in to do the taping. He was doing it as a side job and was there very late at night for about a week. He was finished later than expected and left me with a very short time to get it all painted, but I finished the day of the party. If I hadn't set that deadline, I probably would have taken a month or two longer to get it done. I took some time off from the project until after the New Year, but then it was time to get back to it. You can imagine what my New Year's Resolutions were.

The next phase called for more fun. The house had two bathrooms, one of which was on the way to becoming a basement bathroom. Water had been leaking and rotted the sub-floor leaving the bathtub in danger of falling through. It needed to be entirely gutted. It was actually a pretty easy project. I started by removing everything down to the bare walls. I had to replace a few floor joists and put down a new sub-floor but there were no major surprises. I put in all new fixtures and vinyl flooring. A room that had been the worst in the house was now one of the nicest.

By this time I had been in the house for over a year. When I had time to do things, I didn't have the money, when I had the money I didn't have the time. It was a "Catch 22." It was going slow but the house was getting better and better as I went along. I am an optimist by nature and that is a double-edged sword. It helps you to see and believe what is possible but it also makes you prone to underestimating the time and money that a project requires. When I first bought the house I had figured to be done by now, in reality I was just getting started.

Next I was going to do the main bathroom and the kitchen and dining room as one project. The original kitchen was dark and felt closed in. My plan was to open up the wall between the kitchen and the dining room. I was going to renovate the bathroom as well. To really open things up I was going to create a cathedral ceiling and add skylights. An ambitious project to say the least, but, as they say, in for a penny, in for a pound.

The kitchen design was going to be interesting. In order to save on costs I had jumped at the opportunity to purchase a "demo" kitchen. A local kitchen and bath dealer was moving their showroom and had two of its floor models for sale. The advantage was that these kitchens had every option available so that people could see them when they came to the showroom. They were also being sold at an unbelievably low price. The only problem was that it would be impossible to get any additional cabinets. This meant that I had to change the space to fit the existing configuration instead of the other way around. Of course I didn't think of this before hand and it proved to be quite a challenge.

I was having a hard time trying to come up with a configuration that worked. I was discussing the problem with a friend of mine when I made the observation that things wouldn't be so difficult if the bathroom wasn't where it was. He paused for a moment and said, "Why don't you move it?" The solution was so simple that I couldn't see it: just move the bathroom to another spot. When I figured that part out, everything else just fell into place. This was going to turn the house from a dump into a really nice piece of real estate. It was also going to be a major test of my ability. I would normally tackle plumbing projects myself but for this one I decided to contract it out. Of course it wound up needing more than originally thought, but what else is new? Over budget again!

Like all projects it began with the demolition. As usual, when things were exposed problems were exposed as well. The house was about fifty years old but this part of it had an extension added on about twenty years before. I thought that was good, but no, that was bad. It seems that the extension had been constructed by three guys named Moe, Larry, and Curly. There were all sorts of problems where the new section had been tied into the old. These problems had to be corrected. More time and money!

Eventually the new walls were framed and the skylights were added. The plumbing, gas and sewer lines were roughed in. The drywall was hung and a crew was hired to tape the joints. Things were moving right along. The fixtures went in and the bathroom was functional again. It was time to install the cabinets.

It was here that I hit a snag, the kitchen didn't fit. The kitchen came with a solid surface countertop that was one piece and contained a 45-degree angle at one end. When I tried to place the top on the base cabinets, I was off. I hadn't allowed for the proper overhang. This was inexperience rearing its ugly head. Everything else came out great. The solution wasn't as drastic as I had feared; I had to adjust the size of one wall. It cost me a couple of days and some sheetrock but in the end, it was fine.

As usual, I was over budget. This meant that the flooring had to wait. I had a new kitchen with bare floors. The bathroom had been totally finished but the kitchen and dining room were going to have to be delayed until I came up with more cash. It was probably six months from that point before I was able to complete that part of project.

In time, everything was completed and it turned out to be a good house instead of being the worst house in the town. I learned so much from this rehab. It took a lot longer than expected and cost a lot more than I ever imagined. To spite all of that, it was profitable. Many people would have said "never again" but not me, I enjoyed the sense of accomplishment so much that I couldn't wait to do another project.

I decided to take the lessons t I learned and do it right this time. The first project had been done out of necessity, now I could do it because I wanted to. I knew that if I took what I learned and applied it correctly I could have a very good experience. I now had a very different way of looking at houses. I knew what remodeling and repairs would cost and I had a much better idea of how long things would take. Best of all, I had a game plan.

The real estate market in New York was still very expensive so it was hard work trying to find something that was affordable. Long Island had quite a few foreclosures up for bid each week and I thought that this would be a good way to get a deal. The Federal Government's Housing and Urban Development Agency, or HUD, owned many these homes. The process was simple, each week a list of HUD owned homes was published. The homes were available for inspection for about two weeks prior to the bid date. All of the bids were sealed so you had no way of knowing how much other bidders were offering. It was also a fairly low risk bid in that you only had to put up $1,000 to place a bid. If you lost the bid the money would be returned.

I spent a lot of time looking at these homes. If I felt that a house was a sensible deal I would place a bid. Most of the time I was outbid but I eventually did acquire a HUD home. This house was located in a very nice neighborhood but needed some work. This time the work was not nearly as extensive. Much of it was cosmetic in nature. What had scared people away from this house was standing water in the basement. I had a good idea of where the water was coming from and didn't think it would be a big deal to correct. Turned out I was right.

I purchased the house for $124,000 and paid about $5,000 in closing costs for a total of $129,000. It needed a roof, paint, windows, and carpet, some wood floors needed to be refinished, and one room needed to be gutted and redone. I also decided to put in a new kitchen to further enhance the resale value.

Purchase Price =	$124,000
Closing Costs =	5,000
Total =	$129,000

This project started as they all do: a cleanup and evaluation. I did some basic painting to make it livable. I created my action plan and prioritized the workflow. The job was under way.

The first major item was the roof. I stripped the old roof and made some minor repairs to the roof deck. I began putting down the new shingles and the new roof took shape pretty quickly. At this time I was still doing it the old-fashioned way, hammer and nails. Today I would be using an air powered roofing nail gun. I encountered no major problems and the roof was completed on schedule.

I painted each bedroom and made minor repairs to the walls as needed. The only issue at this point was removing a wall paper border that had been placed on the walls. I used a wall paper steamer but it was still very slow going. I was also replacing the old windows with energy efficient ones as I did each room. Things still went along as expected.

Next up was refinishing the oak flooring in the living room and dining room. For this job I hired a pro. While I probably could have done it, it would have been a first for me. By the time I figured the cost of renting the equipment, buying the material, and the amount of time involved, I thought that it made more sense to contract it out. I left the house for three days and when I came back I had shiny new floors.

Now it was time for the kitchen. I removed everything right down to the bare studs. Then came new insulation, drywall, lighting, cabinets and a floor. I changed the configuration of the kitchen so that it had a more modern appearance and would have more appeal for today's buyer. Once again I was fairly close to my projection of the time needed and I was within my budget.

With the inside completed I was able to move on to the exterior. When I first acquired the house I had to have a massive oak tree removed since it was in danger of falling. Other than that I hadn't done anything on the exterior until now. The house was badly in need of paint and landscaping. These tasks were completed without incident as well. The house was now one of the nicest in the neighborhood.

This job went very smoothly, stayed within the budget, and was a totally different experience than the first house. The explanation for that is quite simple: I learned from the mistakes that I made on the first house. Experience is truly the best teacher. I did not repeat my previous mistakes and I had a much better sense of how to rehab a house.

So how did it work out financially? My cost to purchase the house was $129,000; I added a little more than $15,000 for renovation and repairs. My total cost was just about $144,000. I lived in the house for just over two years and, therefore, avoided capital gains taxes. I was able to sell the house for $300,000 with selling expenses of $21,000. My net profit was $135,000!

Sale Price	=	$300,000
Purchase Cost	=	(129,000)
Renovations	=	(15,000)
Selling Expenses	=	(21,000)
Profit	=	$135,000!

One thing that I did with this house that I hadn't done previously was to keep a record. I took numerous before and after pictures and kept a log of all the expenditures. This made it very easy to see how the project was going. I now do this on all my projects and I can easily refer back to a previous job to see how much something cost and how it ultimately worked out.

After selling this house I moved west to Las Vegas, Nevada. This market was so overheated at the time that finding a good rehab prospect was almost impossible. But through networking connections that I had developed, I learned of a fantastic opportunity in the eastern Nevada town of Ely. This town was a rehabber's paradise. After enduring years of economic stagnation, the town was undergoing a renaissance with a perfect storm of seemingly unrelated events boosting the local economy. A copper mine that had been closed for years was re-opened, an oil field had been discovered to the east, and two major power plants to supply electricity to Reno and Las Vegas were being considered to the north. This sudden growth caused workers to flock to the area and created a housing shortage.

It was such a great area for rehab projects because many homes had been poorly maintained or outright abandoned. A large portion of the housing in the area had been built around 1930. The years of economic decline had led to neglect. The need for housing meant that these projects could be extremely profitable.

I was not alone in my thinking; a rehab boom was underway. Normally my method of operation would be to acquire a house, rehab it and move on. However the competition for houses made me change my ways. I needed to acquire as many properties as quickly as possible before prices rose and rehab candidates disappeared. I literally had an inventory of homes waiting to be rehabbed.

Another thing that happened was that rents rose dramatically because of the shortage of houses available for rent. This caused another shift in strategy; I would hold the houses as rental properties after they were repaired. The high rents provided excellent cash flow and the appreciation potential of the area was fantastic.

The Ely campaign continued for more than two years. The area is still a great opportunity as of today but deals are harder to find. Prices have increased five-fold in some cases. This means that my decision to hold the properties as rentals after rehab was a good one.

I have come to learn that there are always "deals" available. The trick is to separate the good deals from the bad deals. Sometimes market conditions make it easy to find a good deal, other times the conditions make it more difficult. However, good market or bad, the process is always the same. Find a good rehab candidate at a good price and manage the project effectively. If you do that you should make a profit almost every time. Simple, right?

If it were so simple everyone would do it and we would all be multi-millionaires. The unvarnished truth is that the people who think that it's easy wind up getting burned. They don't do their homework and wind up making bad deals. The most common mistakes are paying too much to buy the house, underestimating the cost of repairs needed, underestimating the amount of time the project will take and overestimating the price for which they will be able to sell the house when it is completed.

So how can these mistakes be avoided? By taking the time to learn the business and doing your homework. Experience is indeed the best teacher but that doesn't mean that you should just jump into any deal. Many new investors are so eager to do a deal that they will rationalize negative factors that an experienced investor would spot easily.

The steps can be broken down as follows:

- Find a Rehab Candidate
- Determine if it is a Good Deal
- Make an Offer
- Arrange Financing
- Make Purchase
- Complete Repairs
- Sell Property

Easy right?

Summary

- Determine how much you can invest

- Choose an area to farm

- Do not hesitate to use contractors where needed

- Take pictures

- Keep a project log and journal

A Rehabber's Tale
McGill, Nevada

My first venture into rural Nevada was a purchase I made in the town of McGill, which is about 15 minutes north of Ely. The house had been foreclosed on and was now a bank-owned property or REO. I had been searching the area with an agent and this was one of the first properties we looked at. I was expecting the house to be an absolute horror due to the price. It was listed at $18,000 (no I'm not missing a zero) which is about 6% of what a similar size house was selling for in Las Vegas at the time. I was driving a Ford Expedition that cost almost twice what the house was listed for.

To my surprise the house was not in bad shape. It needed paint, carpet, landscaping, a bathroom makeover and a roof. I estimated I would need $5,000 in repairs. Based on recent area sales of similar houses in the area, the after repair value (ARV) was about $35,000. It was actually fairly easy to get accurate "comps" because all of the houses in the area were almost identical. The town of McGill was built in 1930 as a company town for a mining operation. The company town concept was to build houses for the workers to rent. The lower paid workers would be allowed to rent the smallest homes, middle management could rent larger homes and the nicest homes were reserved for the executives of the company. These homes were grouped by style in different parts of the town and these divisions are still very evident today.

My intention was to hold the property as a rental because demand for housing was strong and rents were very high in relation to price. The house was a two bedroom one-bath model and would be a great rental. While it was very tempting to just pay the asking price and be done with it, I worked with my agent to put together a bid. I submitted an all-cash offer of $16,000 with no contingencies other than an inspection. It turns out that there was one other offer as well but the buyer required a loan and had bad credit. The bank countered my offer and said they would accept $17,000 all-cash. I agreed and we had a deal. Because there was no financing involved the transaction closed fairly quickly.

This was my first time rehabbing a house that was 75 years old. I expected many age-related problems but I was pleasantly surprised to have very few of them. I was actually impressed with the quality that I found in what was a fairly simple house. The heating system and electric had been upgraded within the last ten years and the town had installed a sewer system so I was ahead of the game there. I kept waiting for the other shoe to drop with this house but it never did.

The biggest problem that I encountered was with the roof. I knew that it needed to be replaced immediately. The roof had been redone several times in the 75 years the house had existed but the old roofing had never been stripped. This is fairly common but there was no avoiding the tear-off this time. The typical asphalt shingles that have been used over the years could be expected to last 20–25 years depending on weather conditions. After they have reached the end of their useful life they will start to curl up, break apart and even disintegrate. This roof was long overdue for replacement and was breaking into very small pieces. It is hard work to remove an old roof but generally a fairly simple process. However, when a roof is crumbling it becomes a very tedious and time-consuming endeavor. I have done literally dozens of roof replacements over the years and this was by far the worst. The cleanup crew that I hired to haul away the debris actually said that this was probably the worst that they had ever seen.

Despite all of the problems removing the old roof, installing the new shingles turned out to be a breeze. The roof deck was in surprisingly good shape and the new roof went on quickly. While I was installing the new roof I had a different kind of surprise. A woman holding a baby in her arms came over from across the street and asked me if the house was going to be for rent since her daughter was looking for a place. The baby she was holding was her grandson and it would be very convenient if her daughter lived across the street. I was only half done and I already had a prospective tenant. Plus, how many people can say that they rented a house from the roof? The daughter did not end up renting the house but the mother referred me to someone else who did.

When the roof was complete, I moved on to the bathroom. It was a fairly simple renovation. I removed everything down to the bare studs and started over. The house was going to be a rental so I kept it simple. I installed a new tub, toilet, sink and tub surround, as well as a vinyl floor. I added a mirror, lighting and combination exhaust fan and light. It was a fairly inexpensive project but it wound up looking great. When the bathroom was done it was time for paint, carpet and finishing touches. The exterior needed very little beyond a simple clean up and a little bit of landscaping.

I was done with the project in the expected time frame and I actually came in under budget. My total cost for this house was about $22,000 which included the purchase, closing costs and materials for renovation. I did the entire project myself with the exception of carpet installation and debris removal. The house has been rented since it was complete for $600 per month, which is almost 3% of the purchase price. I recently had the property appraised and I was pleased to learn that it is worth $60,000 only two years later. That's a deal I'll take any day!

Chapter 2

Before You Begin

The starting point of all achievement is desire.
—Napoleon Hill

You probably can't wait to get going. You're ready to buy a house and rip down walls and make a fortune flipping property. That's a recipe for disaster; you need to prepare yourself first. When a skyscraper is constructed the builder starts by laying the proper foundation, you must do the same.

Personal Finances

Research from the U.S. Bureau of Labor Statistics shows that the majority of start-up businesses will fail in the early years of their existence. The failure rate is between 70% and 80% in the first year, with only half of the remaining business still in operation after 5 years. The overwhelming reason for these failures is poor planning and lack of money to sustain operations. Your rehabbing business is no different.

Perhaps you are planning to finance the entire purchase and rehab, so you feel that you don't have to worry about the money. But what about your personal bills? You still need to pay for your own living expenses; they aren't going to go away. If you have a regular job you might think that things will just go on as they always have. You will probably find, however, that you have many additional expenses that aren't included in the financing that you've arranged, how will you handle those?

Reserves

You need to be sure that you have ample *reserves* to handle the unexpected. In rehab it is almost certain that things will take longer than you expected and cost more than you thought. You handle this by having a sufficient amount of money set aside to cover these contingencies. If you think that a project will be finished and sold in three months then you should plan on it taking six months or more. If you feel that your budget for renovations is accurate then you may want to pad that amount by 10%, if it is an older property with a potential for a lot of surprises then you may want to factor in 25%. The larger the reserve fund the safer you are.

Even veteran rehabbers get caught in a bind. They may have completed multiple projects just as the market softened and are now unable to sell them. They may need to place tenants in the properties until the market improves. Having sufficient reserves will allow them to handle any negative cash flow that they may have.

How much you need will vary based on your individual situation. How long would the money last if you were unable to sell the house? If you have a job and lost it how long would it be until you are in real financial trouble? Many people will rely on credit cards or credit lines to help them through a tight spot. The problem with using these is that they can have a high interest cost and you must make payments. If your budget is already strained these payments will only make it worse. Obviously cash is best, you do not need to add payments to your budget and the cost is just the interest that you don't earn by having it in the bank.

Start by figuring out your current reserves. How much cash do you have on hand? How much credit is available at low interest rates, home equity, 401(k) loans etc.? How much money could you borrow quickly at higher interest rates? What would the repayment terms be on these options? You may think that you won't ever need these reserves but you still need to be aware of what you have in case you ever do.

If you do not have much in the way of reserves you may wish to place your plans on hold until you have a fund built up. If you do not have credit lines or credit cards for emergencies you should try to get them. If you are employed you may want to consider a part-time job for a while in order to establish a reserve account. Rehab projects have a way of draining cash quickly; you need to be properly prepared.

Income Streams

You may have heard the term "multiple streams of income." Simply put, an *income stream* is a source of money that you receive on a regular basis. Theses streams can come from many different sources that are totally independent from one another. The most obvious one would be from W-2 income that you receive on a job. If you have a spouse who is also employed then that would be a second stream since it exists independently of the first. Do you earn interest on a bank account? That would be another income stream, as would earnings from a mutual fund or other investments, income from a part-time job, business earnings, rental income, royalties, earnings from a network marketing business and so on.

Some income streams may be small, and others large, but they all count. You are in great financial shape if any one of those streams could be removed without changing your overall financial picture greatly. This is not usually the case for most people. Most potential investors tend to rely heavily on one stream such as a job or business. When you get to the point that you are not dependent on any particular income stream you are well on your way to financial independence, if not already there.

The goal of many rehabbers and real estate investors is to create these multiple streams. Some income may be derived from flipping properties after they've been rehabbed while holding others as long-term investments. A typical strategy may be to hold one property as a long-term rental for every two or three projects completed. Some properties are better rental candidates while others should be flipped for immediate profit; you need to evaluate this on a case by case basis.

Goals

Numerous studies have shown that people who set goals are more successful than people who do not. People who write their goals down routinely achieve more than those who don't. People have a tendency to be very vague about goals. They'll say things like "I want to be a millionaire," or "I want to be rich," or "I want to have a great life," but they don't ever define what that means. Goals should be carefully thought out. It is helpful to follow the **SMART** system for setting goals, which first appeared in *The One Minute Manager,* by Ken Blanchard and Spenser Johnson. If you apply this system to your goal setting you have a much greater likelihood of achieving those goals.

There are several variations of the SMART system, but they are similar, and will help you to set clearly defined goals for your business. Goal setting also works well in your personal life and can help you to set and achieve goals in many different ways. If you have never set goals you should try it and see the difference that it can make. Your goals should be written down and reviewed frequently and you should keep them someplace where you will see them. It also helps to share them with others. By telling people what you hope to achieve you are making a commitment and are much more likely to stick to your goals.

Think **SMART** when setting goals:

Specific: Goals should be as specific as possible and have a date by which you plan to achieve them. If it is vague and undated it is merely a wish.

Meaningful: What is your **"why"**? If a goal has no real meaning for you there is little likelihood that you will achieve it.

Attainable: A goal should not be too easy; you should have to stretch to achieve it. However, the bar should not be set so high that you have no hope of reaching it.

Realistic: While you may be able to attain your goals, are they realistic when viewed along with other aspects of your life?

Trackable: Can your goals be tracked so that you know how you are doing?

Your goals should be taken very seriously and not be treated the way that most people treat their New Year's Resolutions.

Dream Map

There is amazing power in the mind's subconscious. You are con-stantly picking up signals that you are not aware of. You can use this power to your advantage by giving your mind powerful suggestions. Many people have embraced the technique of creating a dream board or vision board. The idea is simple but very effective. The idea is to place visual images of things that you would like to acquire or goals that you would like to achieve. You place the board someplace where you will see it several times a day and you mind will subconsciously absorb these images. Without even realizing it you will move towards these goals.

Dreams to Reality Map

Start with a 16x20 picture frame.

Place a family photo in the center.

Use pictures from brochures, magazines, etc., to illustrate things that you would like to have, places you would like to go or goals you would like to achieve.

Add inspirational or motivational quotes.

IMPORTANT—hang it someplace where you will see it every day

I first tried this technique about 15 years ago and I have had amazing results. A business associate who had started using the idea himself introduced me to the technique. He had a number of people gather at his printing shop to put together dream boards of their own. I didn't really embrace the idea at the time but I went for the socializing and pizza that went along with it. After putting the board together I took it home and hung it up as we were instructed to. I paid little attention to it but I did walk by it several times each day. After about a year something made me look at it and I realized that of the ten things on the board I had achieved all but one of them. The things that I put on there were not things that I would have ordinarily expected to achieve, yet they happened. I have been using a dream board ever since, I create a new one at the start of every year and update it a couple of times as the year progresses.

Psychology of Rehab

You may be thinking what does psychology have to do with swinging a hammer and rehabbing houses? It has absolutely nothing to do with swinging a hammer but it has a lot to do with rehabbing houses. What you will be doing primarily is dealing with people. You have people that you are buying from and people that you are selling to. You also have to deal with various contractors, salespeople, partners, employers, employees, relatives and your spouse. Most of all you have to deal with yourself and your own emotions, skills and limitations. A little knowledge of the psychology involved can go a long way.

Many people get into rehabbing houses because they feel that it is an easy way to make money. They watch TV shows or read books that make it seem that anyone can do it. Some people jump right in and learn as they go along while others spend time doing painstaking research on the whole process. What few people do, however, is to look at themselves to see if this is a venture for which they are suited.

Rehabbing property will put you through many ups and downs and psychological twists and turns. Not everyone is able to deal with this effectively. It is important to do a self-evaluation to see if this is something that you should attempt.

Personality Types

While everyone has a unique personality, in each person there is one personality type that will be dominant. There are many variations on the theme, but it all boils down to four different categories. You will see it broken down in many different ways with many different sub-types, but it still comes down to four major styles. Some theories focus on behavior or learning styles, while others focus on the underlying motivation of the individual. The different theories are all basically valid they just have different ways of working with the same information.

The more important aspect of the personality types is how they interact with one another. Some styles work very well together while others clash. We've all seen the flip-and-grow-rich TV shows where friends partner up to do a deal and wind up in a state of perpetual conflict. Two personality types who do very well as friends may do very poorly as business partners. Having an understanding of the different styles can help you understand how to work with people who have a different style than you do.

The Driver

We all know people that we would call a "Type A," or *driver*, personality. This is the hard-charging, intense, no-nonsense individual who is always working to be the best. The driver is a results-oriented, bottom line kind of person. They are not looking for a lot of fluff; they are direct and to the point. This personality type enjoys a challenge and is not afraid of taking risks in order to reach a goal. The driver is persistent, focused and decisive.

The down side to the driver personality is that they are great starters but are usually looking to move on before they have finished what they are working on. They are always looking ahead and hate routine. The driver is prone to just jumping right in without thinking everything through. They can be perceived as arrogant and uncaring because of their relentless determination to get where they are going.

The driver is often found in management positions, commissioned sales and business owners. Their primary motivation is power or being in charge. Above all the driver wants to win.

Expressive

Everyone knows that person who is the life of the party, which would be the *expressive* personality type. The social butterfly always seems to be the center of attention and people love to be around them. These people love a party and like to be in group settings. They tend to be talkative and outgoing and love having a good time. They are generally supportive of others and good team players.

The negative part of this personality type is that it's all about them. They need to have the spotlight and are always worried about what people think of them. It is not unusual for this type to take it personally if they feel that someone doesn't like them. They may have a hard time focusing on the task at hand because they are more interested in having fun than getting the job done.

This type is often found in sales positions, party planning, travel, advertising, and they are usually good public speakers and are often found in politics. They are motivated by fun and have a need to be liked.

Friend

The *friend* is that person that you can always count on when you need them. They are reliable, punctual, and consistent and can be counted on to follow the rules and procedures. They are content to have a routine and guidelines to follow. They are good team players and usually exhibit a high degree of compassion.

However, they hate change or anything that is out of the ordinary. They tend to be passive and tolerant. This tolerance can lead to a blow-up if they reach the limits of what they can quietly take. They will be agreeable even if they don't agree just to maintain peace and harmony. It's hard to know what this personality type is really thinking.

This individual will often be employed in retail or service positions. Peace and harmony motivate this person and the primary need is for security.

Analytical

The *analytical* personality is the proverbial bean counter. They are extremely detail oriented and will check and re-check their answers just to be sure that they are correct. This personality type is generally very serious and puts accuracy above everything else. Everything they do has a logical order, which in turn makes them consistent and predictable. They tend to be patient and loyal and you can count on them to do the job right. You can count on them to be neat and to be precise in everything that they do.

This personality type is probably the reason for the phrase "paralysis by analysis." They tend to overanalyze things in order to be sure that everything is correct. They do not make quick decisions and see a deadline as secondary to being right about the facts. They can be emotional and very sensitive, especially if they were wrong about something.

The analytical type is generally your accountant, actuary, engineer or computer programmer. They can also be very good at technical sales or other positions involving numbers. They are motivated by intimacy and have an overriding need to be right.

Interacting

Understanding the different personality types can help you in all aspects of your life. You should realize that everyone has traits of all the different types but one type will tend to dominate. No one type is better than the other, they are just different. What is really important is to understand how the different personalities interact. In your rehab business you will be dealing with many different people. Understanding them can help you work well with people who may have a very different style than you do.

Certain personality types work very well together while others will tend to clash. When you look at the box below you see the different types in certain positions. The top boxes (analytical and driver) are people who tend to be focused on tasks while the bottom two (friend and social) tend to be focused on people.

Analytical	Driver
Friend	Expressive

The personality types that are diagonally across from each other will have a tendency to clash. This does not mean that they can't work together but they will have more difficulty understanding and relating to one another. The styles on the right side will tend to be aggressive when faced with a confrontational situation and the ones on the left will lean towards being passive. These are just some basic tendencies; everyone has their own unique style since everybody is a blend of all of the different types.

This is not meant to be an in-depth psychological discussion. The idea is to make you aware of the differences that you will encounter when dealing with people. If you learn how to interact with all the different styles, you can be much more effective in your business and personal life. The first step is to figure out what type you are and how you relate to other personality types. There are numerous resources to be found on this topic and if you take some time to learn more about it you should find it to be a great benefit.

Personal Coach

Tiger Woods is considered by many to currently be the best golfer in the world, maybe of all time. Yet he still has a coach to help keep him on track. Having a coach can be a major benefit to you as well. You can use a professional or a trusted friend or mentor to work with you as you strive to reach your goals. The coach's job is not to be your buddy, or yes man, but to be brutally honest with you. For this reason you might find a professional success coach to be more objective.

The job of the coach is not to be a therapist or shrink, but to be your guide. Their aim is to get the most out of the ability that you do have and to get you to stretch beyond your limits in order to attain greater success. A professional coach is trained to help you get past the obstacles that may be holding you back.

Partner or Solo?

Are you intending to do this business on your own or will you have a partner? Which way you go can have a major impact on the overall outcome. There are advantages and disadvantages to each. Your personality type is a big factor in this decision. Are you someone who likes to go it alone or do you prefer to have someone to work with?

The advantage to having a partner is that you have someone to share the workload. Your partner may have capital to contribute to the venture or have knowledge that can be a vital asset to the business. A partner gives you someone to share ideas with and gives you someone to turn to when things don't go according to plan.

The disadvantage to working with a partner is that you might not work well together. If your personalities clash it could be a very rocky road. A lot of people get into trouble by going into business with friends. Two people who have a very good friendship could make a very bad business partnership. If one partner finds himself contributing most of the money or doing the bulk of the work it could create bad feelings between the two.

If you do choose to work with a partner, you should have things spelled out in writing. The more detailed the agreement the better the chance for success. One of the most important things is for each partner to understand his role and responsibilities to the partnership. When everything is spelled out in great detail there is a much smaller chance for misunderstandings. Things should never be assumed, they should be discussed.

Summary

- Take Stock of Personal Finances

- Have Sufficient Reserves

- Look to Create Multiple Streams of Income

- Set *SMART* Goals

- Create Dream Map

- Learn Your Personality Type

- Consider a Personal Coach

- Decide Whether to Partner or Go Solo

A Rehabber's Tale
McGill Nevada #2

As I got more involved in the Ely, Nevada market I started developing contacts in the area. One of these contacts alerted me to a house that was coming on the market in the town of McGill. It was a two bedroom, one bath house that was in decent shape. The owner lived out of state and was looking to unload the property. The home was being listed with a local real estate agent at a price that was well below the values in the area. I had my agent in Ely contact the listing agent for the details. The numbers looked good so I thought it was worth checking into.

Since I was located 250 miles away, I had my agent take a look. She felt that it was an excellent buy that would not last long and that I had to see it myself. The house was actually being listed that very day and I felt that I needed to move quickly. The following day I drove for four hours in order to look at the house with my own eyes. I met my agent and as we went to see the property I was pleasantly surprised. Based on the price, I assumed that it was going to need quite a bit of rehab work. What I found was that it needed a roof repair, some paint and a new shower in the bathroom. My estimate was that it needed less than $2,000 worth of work and about ten days of time to have it ready for rent.

I was intrigued by the house because of the price. Similar houses were going for over $40,000 yet this one was listed for $28,000. I made an offer of $26,000 immediately and I included contingencies for inspection and financing as my escape clauses. The offer was accepted and I had the house under contract. By the time this was done the house had been on the market for less than 24 hours. Had I hesitated it probably would have been sold to someone else in a matter of days.

There were so many potential deals that I was evaluating at the time that I was reluctant to tie up any cash. I had learned that Countrywide would make loans as small as $20,000 while most lenders would be reluctant to do anything below $50,000. I had never attempted to get a mortgage for such a low amount but I figured that I would give it a shot. My application was approved almost instantly pending a favorable review of the title and an appraisal. I thought I was home free.

It was here that I hit a snag. There is a very different dynamic when working in a small town. Apparently there were only a couple of appraisers in the area and they were very careful about their work. The appraiser had no problem establishing the value but noted the condition of the roof. When the lender received the report they insisted on a roof inspection by a licensed roofing contractor. In a small town there was essentially only one roofing contractor who could do this inspection, therefore he could expect to get any work that might be needed. Of course, his report noted that the house would not be habitable without having the work done.

The lender insisted that the roof had to be repaired in order for them to fund the loan and the repair had to be made by a licensed roofing contractor. I had estimated that I could do the repair myself for $250 but I went ahead and got the contractor's estimate. You can imagine my surprise when the estimate came in at $3,000! The lender would not allow me to do the repair on my own but they would hold the repair money in escrow so that I could have it done after I closed.

I'm sure the contractor thought he had this deal in the bag since I couldn't get the loan without it. There was no way that I was going to pay ten times what it would cost me to do it myself. I told the lender to forget about the loan and I used cash to make the purchase. While I didn't get the money I was looking for I did learn a good lesson. I learned about the difficulty and expense of doing small loans. Many of the fees and costs associated with obtaining a mortgage are very similar regardless of the loan amount. This means that those fees are significantly higher as a percentage of the amount borrowed on smaller loans.

I ultimately purchased the home and completed the rehab. I was under budget and kept to my timeline. I had a tenant in the house less than 30 days after I closed escrow. The house has been rented to the same tenant the entire time that I have owned it. My total cost for purchase and rehab was $28,000 and it is rented for $550 per month. A recent appraisal put the value at $68,000 just 18 months later. This turned out to be another great deal because I acted fast.

Chapter 3

Types of Rehabs

Luck is the residue of design.
—**Branch Rickey, Baseball GM**

Residential rehabs tend to fall into four different categories: personal use, rental, flip and absentee. Each type has its own characteristics and what you do in terms of work is different for each one. Let's explore each of these.

Personal Use

Many people get started in rehabbing properties by fixing up a house for their own use. I started just this way, I needed a place that I could afford and a fixer was just the ticket. When you buy a house that needs work you are going to be able to acquire it for substantially less than the market value of a house in the same neighborhood that is in excellent condition. The work you put into it becomes your *sweat equity*. Perhaps you are taking the step from renting to owning and this is a way to buy something that is affordable to you.

Rehabbing can also be a way to purchase a house in a neighborhood that you might not be able to afford otherwise. You may have a choice between buying a nice house in an area that is not too bad or a house in a great part of town that needs some work. I can tell you from experience that you will be a hit with the neighbors if you take the eyesore of the block and turn it into a nice house.

When you are buying the house for your own personal use you will not face the time constraints that you might if you needed to do a quick flip. Once you have fixed it to the point that it is livable you can work at a pace that is comfortable to you. You can also do things to the house that suit your taste without having as much concern about the end buyer. Of course, you want to be able to sell it eventually but you can do things to the house that suit your lifestyle.

Another advantage of buying a fixer for your own use is that you may be able to avoid taxes when you sell. Current law allows you to exclude from your income a significant amount of any gain in a property used as your own home. Presently the law allows single taxpayers to exclude $250,000 in gains and married couples can exclude up to $500,000 provided that you have used the house as your personal residence for two of the last five years. I know several people who have flipped themselves to better and better houses every two years. With several flips like this you could find yourself living in your dream home.

If you have never rehabbed before, this is an excellent way to gain experience. You learn the most from your mistakes (and you will make plenty when you begin.) When you make a mistake on a house you are living in it is usually not as bad as a mistake that you make in a house you intend to flip. If you are trying to flip time is a crucial element, every mistake that costs you time will also cost you in terms of profit. Time isn't as crucial if the house is also your home. You do not have the additional carrying cost in your own home. If you are intending to flip a house you have the carrying cost on that house as well as the costs of your own home. This added cost magnifies every mistake and every delay in the timeline.

Rental

When you rehab a house in order to rent it you will usually do it differently than if you plan to sell it. Most renters will not take care of a property as well as they would if they owned it. Even if you carefully screen your tenants you can expect to have problems. Many of my rehabs are held as rentals and I don't rehab them as extensively as if I were planning on selling. When you are going to rent the house, you only need to do the work to make it acceptable to a tenant, not to attract a buyer.

If I am rehabbing to rent I view the project in two stages. The first stage is to do enough to make it a quality rental. The second stage is done when I've decided to sell the house. This is the point at which I will put in higher quality upgrades that will help to sell the house. In stage one I'll use basic carpet and tile and I don't do anything fancy. Prior to sale I'll spend some time to do the things that are important to a buyer.

When I buy a house that is in need of major renovation, I will rarely rent it. You don't want to do a major rehab job over again because a tenant destroyed it. If I find a property that only needs a small amount of work to make it tenant ready, I will consider renting it. When a tenant moves I then have the option of finding a new tenant or completing the rehab and selling it. There can be tax advantages to doing this, a short term hold will result in the gains being taxed as ordinary income but if you hold it for a year or more it is treated as a long-term capital gain. Long-term capital gains are taxed at a much lower rate than ordinary income.

Another advantage when rehabbing to rent instead of flipping is that you can wait for the market to be in a position that favors a seller. Real estate, like any investment market, moves in cycles. Sometimes it is a buyer's market, sometimes a seller's market, and at other times the market is neutral. If you can afford to hold a property as a rental, you can sell when market conditions favor the seller. You may also benefit from appreciation in prices. I try to hold properties as rentals if a market is experiencing price appreciation and the prospects for further gains exist.

Holding property long term is the key to creating wealth in real estate. The sweat equity that you gain from rehabbing is only part of the equation. Over time you get the benefit of price appreciation and you also have the benefit of the mortgage principal being reduced. The rent that the property generates means that the tenants are actually helping you pay the mortgage and build your net worth.

The 1% Myth

What makes a profitable rental? You may have heard of the 1% rule, which means that a property should have a monthly rent equal to 1% of the purchase price in order to be profitable. If you follow this rule you will probably be losing money. Expenses will vary by region, some areas have higher property taxes or insurance rates so no rule is absolute. However, national statistics show that you can expect expenses to consume 40–50% of your gross rents. Expenses include taxes, insurance, utilities, property management fees, maintenance, and administrative and miscellaneous expenses.

Let's say we purchase a house for $100,000 that can be rented for $1,000 per month or 1% of the purchase price.

Rent	$1,000
Taxes	(100)
Insurance	(50)
Property Management	(100)
Utilities	(75)
Maintenance and Repair	(100)
Administrative & Miscellaneous	(25)
Net Rent	$550

The net rent would also be known as the *net operating income* or NOI.

In this example expenses were 45% of the gross rent. The numbers used are typical of what you can expect. Some areas, like Texas, may have higher insurance rates and other areas, like Long Island, NY, will have much higher property taxes. In that case your net rent will be even lower.

If you paid cash for the house you will net $6600 per year or 6.6% on your investment. Most people don't pay cash when they buy a house. If you obtained a mortgage with a 20% down payment and an interest rate of 7-½ % for 30 years you would have a payment of $559.37. This means that you have a negative cash flow of $9.37 per month or $112.46 per year. So by investing $20,000 you have the privilege of losing $112.46 each year!

The reality is that most loans for investment properties are going to have an interest rate higher that 7-½ %. Many investors want to put down as little as possible which means your cash flow may be even worse. Smaller down payments may also mean that you need to pay PMI charges, which further reduce cash flow.

The 1% rule was probably created by real estate agents or the sellers of investment properties in order to make a property look like a better investment. Many people will ignore management fees because they intend to manage the property themselves. That is like working for free, the fee still needs to be calculated even if you intend to earn that fee yourself. Administrative expenses are often overlooked or ignored all together. These fees are real and should be included. You still have to pay your accountant or attorney, buy office supplies and travel to and from the property on occasion. These expenses exist whether you acknowledge them or not.

The vacancy factor is another expense that tends to be minimized. It is frequently shown as a low number, like 5%, that is generally unrealistic. A 5% vacancy is a little more than two weeks out of the year. When a tenant moves out of a property it almost always takes a month or more to have a new tenant move in. After an existing tenant moves out you need to inspect the property and perform any required maintenance. You may need to paint, clean the carpets and do other things to get it ready for the next tenant. The house needs to be marketed to attract a new tenant and a prospective renter should be screened. This all takes time. You may find yourself going through the screening process only to have someone back out at the last minute because they found something they liked better. When that happens, you have to start all over again. For this reason I use a minimum of 10% for a vacancy factor, even in a strong rental market. If the rental market isn't strong you may want to use an even higher vacancy factor. If you experience a vacancy rate of less than 10% consider yourself lucky. Any agent that suggests that 5% is reasonable has probably never owned a rental property.

The biggest expense that is often understated is maintenance and repair. It is a variable expense that will be very small at times but very large at other times, such as when you need to replace a major item like a furnace or roof. The best way to handle these expenses is to have a reserve fund set aside to handle the repairs as they come up. I like to set aside 10% every month in a separate fund to cover repairs as they are needed. If you only have one or two properties you may get lucky and not have any major expenses. However, the more properties that you own the more things that you will need to take care of. Even if you handle the maintenance yourself it needs to be figured in your calculations.

Remember, if you are using a down payment to get the property to provide a positive cash flow it is not really a true positive cash flow. You need to calculate the return that you are getting on that down payment … this would be the cash-on-cash return. If you put down $10,000 to get a $100 per month cash flow, your cash-on-cash return is 12%.

```
$10,000 Invested

Return = $100 per month

$100 x 12 months = $1200

$1200/$10,000 = 12%
```

To properly evaluate a property as a rental you must calculate it as if you were putting nothing down. After that you can calculate the effects of a down payment on your return. You need to use realistic assumptions for mortgage rates as well. Interest rates for investments properties are higher than for owner occupied homes yet you will see salespeople using the lower rates to show better cash flow.

Let's try an example with numbers that are fairly typical.

Assumptions:

Purchase Price = $100,000

Mortgage Interest Rate = 8.75%

Payment = $787 for 30 Years

PMI = $63

Total payment = $850

Taxes	$125
Insurance	50
Utilities	75
Maintenance	10%
Miscellaneous	5%
Property Management	10%

Fixed Expenses = $250 per month

Variable Expenses = 25% of rent

In this example we have fixed expenses of $250 per month no matter what the rent is. We also have expenses that will total 25% of the rent itself. So we have a payment of $850 and fixed expenses of $250 for a total of $1,100 per month ($850 + 250 = $1,100). We know that our variable expenses are 25% of the rent, which means that we get to keep 75% of the rent before fixed expenses.

Now we are able to calculate our break-even point. We need to take the total amount of fixed expenses and divide it by the percentage of net rent collected. This will give us the amount of rent needed to break-even.

$1,100/75% = $1,467

Rent needed to break-even = $1,467

If you want to earn a minimum profit of $100 per month you need to add that to the break-even figure. In this case you would need a monthly rent of almost $1,600 to earn your desired profit. That figure would total 1.6% of the purchase price.

Let's get back to the 1% myth. At 1% the rent on this $100,000 would be $1,000, how would that work out?

Rent =	$1,000
Variable Expenses (25%)	(250)
Fixed Expenses	(250)
NOI	500
Mortgage	(850)
Net Income = ($350)	

So much for the 1% rule!

So how do we calculate the effect of a down payment? We start with the figures that were determined using a nothing down strategy. We then take the improvement in the cash flow that would be realized by using a down payment and multiply it by 12 to give us an annual amount. We divide that amount by the amount invested to give us an annual percentage return on our down payment.

Let's go back to our example and assume a 10% down payment. This would give us a loan amount of $90,000 and reduce our payment to $708. We have improved our cash flow by $79 ($787 - 708 = $79) per month or $948 per year. We divide $948 by the $10,000 investment, which gives us an annual return of 9.48%. This does not make the investment any more or less profitable; it just shows the effect of a down payment on your cash flow. In the 1% example you would still be losing money, you are just losing $79 less each month.

How much of a down payment to put down depends on your investment objectives. The important thing to remember is that when you make a down payment in order to achieve a certain cash flow you are actually buying that cash flow with your down payment. Don't be fooled into thinking that a property has a positive cash flow because you made a large down payment. Always calculate the true cash flow as if you are putting nothing down.

So if the 1% rule is a myth, what should you use as a rule of thumb? That number will vary based on certain expenses in your geographical target area. If taxes, insurance and other expenses are very high you must use a higher number, if those expenses are low you can get away with a lower one. You should evaluate a number of properties to get an idea as to what works in your area. I use 1.5% as my screen. If a property will rent for 1.5% or more of the purchase price I will take a closer look. Most properties that I look at that are at the 1.5% mark will not work but they are close enough to deserve a more detailed evaluation. I can always make an offer to purchase a property at a number that will work and move on if the offer isn't accepted. If it is below the 1.5% number I will immediately rule the property out the majority of the time. The number that you use as a screening tool will vary depending on where you are. There are many people who will use a 2% criteria because the area they are in has higher expenses. The screen is meant to give you a basic idea, it is not a substitute for doing your homework.

Most major cities will not come close to this screening number. Places like Los Angeles, San Francisco, Las Vegas, and New York City are lucky to have numbers approaching a rent to price ratio of ½%. The only way to get cash flow here is to buy with a large down payment. In markets like this you have a much better chance for profit doing rehabs that you will flip than by trying to make it on rental income.

Flip

Most rehabbers renovate houses with the intention of flipping them for quick profits. In this scenario you will do the work with the idea of maximizing the resale value. When fixing to flip you always need to keep the buyer in mind. Many people have a tendency to incorporate their own taste into the project. This is fine if your taste is what the average buyer in that neighborhood would want. If your taste runs in a different direction you could have difficulty when trying to sell. In most cases you want to stick with neutral colors and conservative design choices. This will help to keep the pool of potential buyers as large as possible.

When you are rehabbing to flip you must carefully consider the market conditions to determine if this is a viable strategy. Many markets that were a flipper's dream a short time ago are now a flipper's nightmare. If you intend to flip in a soft market you must have a strategy. Your property needs to be nicer than the competition and should ideally be priced below competing homes. If the market is soft you should try to understand why so that you will have a better idea as to what it might take to get a home sold. Houses sell in even the slowest market if they are priced right.

Real estate is very much a local market. National trends always have an effect but local factors will always carry more weight. Even when the national real estate scene is showing large declines you will have areas that are appreciating. If you are investing in these areas of local appreciation you can do very well in spite of the national market.

If you are in a slow or declining market you can take advantage of these conditions by getting a better price when you buy. You need to acquire the property at a low enough price so that you can complete the rehab and still sell at a price low enough to attract buyers. Remember that you make your profit when you buy; you realize your gain when you sell. If you stick with that philosophy you should rarely get hurt and any appreciation that you do get will be icing on the cake.

When renovating for a quick sale you need to pay close attention to your timeline. Every day that you own the property is reducing your profit. If the market has been trending down you may be losing value even faster. You should also avoid holding out for top dollar when selling. Many rehabbers have rejected offers because they were too low only to find that they made less money by waiting for a better offer to come along.

Absentee

Another type of rehab that is growing in popularity is the hands-off or absentee rehab. While this has been around for a long time, it has generally been in the form of an investor in one area that invests in another area through someone that they know and trust. However larger companies are getting involved because of the profit potential.

The business model of companies specializing in absentee rehabs is somewhat unique in that they handle all aspects of the transaction for the investor and provide certain guarantees as well. One such company is *Blue Moon Capital* (BMC) in Denver. They target neighborhoods that are experiencing what they call "pocket appreciation," which is usually an area within a city that is rising in quality and value. What they do is acquire properties that have been foreclosed on by lenders. Then they evaluate these properties and determine the scope of work that is needed. They contract with an investor who supplies a small down payment and acquires the property. BMC also provides the rehab financing and sells the property to the investor at the completion of the project. The twist is that they guarantee to sell at 80% of the appraised value. They will only work with seasoned investors who intend to hold the properties for a period of time in order to allow the entire neighborhood to appreciate.

The advantage to the investor is that they are getting a property that has been completely rehabbed at a price that is equal to 80% of appraised value. They have none of the headaches of doing the rehab nor do they take on the risk of cost overruns and unexpected problems.

It is a completely turnkey investment. The disadvantage is that they are expected to hold the property for a period of time so that the area can appreciate in value. If the properties were sold to investors who intended to do short-term flips there would be so many properties for sale in the area that it would be difficult for anyone to make money.

Not everyone is suited to absentee rehabs. There are many pitfalls associated with this scenario. If you are dealing with companies that are not reputable you could wind up making very poor investments. If this is something that you are inclined to do, you should do your homework to be sure that you are making a solid investment.

I have also come across real estate agents that are knowledgeable in rehab properties. They work with investors from other areas to help them acquire properties that are suitable rehab projects. They also arrange for the rehab work to be done and, in some cases, actually manage the project. When the project is complete they handle the sale or help place the house with a property manager so that it can be rented. If you are inclined to do this you should interview the agent carefully and speak to other clients that they have already worked with.

Choosing a Strategy

As you can see, there are many types of rehab. You need to choose a strategy that is a good fit for your situation. Not everyone can afford to hold a property as a rental or is willing to take on the risk associated with an absentee rehab. You need to choose the path that makes the most sense for you. Whatever path you ultimately choose still involves the same steps. You need to find the right property at the right price and rehab it for maximum profit.

Shall we get started?

Summary

- Determine what type of rehab to do:

- Personal use

- Rental

- Flip

- Absentee

A Rehabber's Tale

Ruth

Ruth is an old mining town in the Ely, Nevada area. The community's fortunes are closely tied to the operation of the mine. The town was built in 1930 as a company town for the workers. The houses are mostly small and simple in style. The area went through a severely depressed period economically when the mine closed. Many houses were abandoned and most of the others fell into a state of disrepair. But fortune smiled on Ruth when the mine was purchased and re-opened by a major mining conglomerate. The town slowly came back to life.

On one trip to the Ely area I decided to look at some properties in Ruth. I came across one house that was for sale at $45,000. Similar houses were selling for about $65,000 so I thought it was worth a look. I expected it to be one of the run down houses in the area but I was surprised to find that it was in fairly good shape. I made arrangements to look at it the next day.

The outside had been freshly painted and the landscaping looked good. The roof was in poor enough shape to require replacement, but it wasn't a total disaster. The inside was in great shape and didn't need much in the way of repairs. I felt like I was missing something because it was in great condition for the price.

I did some investigating and found that an older, retired couple owned the house. They had purchased the property as a retirement home but found it to be too small. They purchased a larger home in the same area and needed to sell this one. I learned that they bought the home for about $30,000 a little more than a year before. I had hoped to get the property for about $40,000 so I made an offer of $38,000 asking the owners to credit me with $2,000 for repairs. They countered with $38,000 and a repair credit of $500 and I accepted. I essentially purchased the home for $37,500.

The key to the deal was that I was a cash buyer and offered to close as fast as they could complete the paperwork. My efforts to find out why they wanted to sell allowed me to make an offer that would appeal to them. The fast close was more important than the price. They still had a nice profit in the short time that they owned the house but they were able to get rid of it and go on with their life.

I expected to have a pretty quick turn-around on the rehab so I instructed my property manager to start locating a tenant. The roof turned out to be a little more difficult than I expected since I needed to remove a non-functional chimney and make some repairs to the roof deck, but it was still done in a timely manner. The other work that was needed was all minor and completed quickly.

The total repair cost on this house was only $1500. My total investment including repairs and purchase came to just about $40,000 and I was able to rent it for $550 per month. It was a quick and easy deal, and I now have about $25,000 of equity in the property since it is worth around $65,000. It is in an area that is showing strong appreciation as it rebounds from years of economic despair and should be a great investment in both the short-term as well as the long-term.

Chapter 4

Evaluating a Property

*There is a wisdom of the head, and a wisdom
of the heart.*—**Charles Dickens**

What is a good rehab candidate? In looking for a deal you want to find
the proverbial "worst house in a good neighborhood." That is not to
say that you are looking for something that is falling down. You are
looking for a property that is not on a par with the neighborhood standards with the goal of rehabbing the property so that it is in line with
other houses in the area. What you do not want to do is exceed those
standards by any great degree because you probably will not get a fair
return on any additional investment.

Structure

The first thing to look at is the structure itself. Are there major
structural problems? If so, the cost of correcting these deficiencies
could make it difficult to obtain a reasonable profit. These problems
could include a crumbling foundation, soil issues, poorly constructed
additions, severe termite or carpenter ant damage to name a few. While

these are items that can all be dealt with, they have to be taken into consideration when evaluating the project as a whole.

There are many different types of foundations that you will find. Concrete slab, poured concrete, and concrete block are the most common. Some parts of the country even have redwood foundations. Wood in contact with the ground is usually an invitation to termite infestation but redwood seems to be impervious to insects. When looking at poured concrete you should be watching out for cracking and crumbling. With concrete block you should pay attention to the mortar lines to see if there are large gaps. If the floors are sagging or have too much bounce you may be dealing with foundation issues.

Another major issue is water. Is there water in the basement or crawl-space? This is a problem that can be overcome but it can't be ignored. I have been able to get a couple of very good deals because of water issues that other people were afraid to deal with. A structure with a history of water infiltration will tend to have many problems. The wood will tend to warp and a cycle of cooling and thawing can cause major damage. When looking at a house with foundation or water problems you need to be extremely cautious. The problems may be more trouble than it is worth.

Is the structure of the building itself acceptable? If the original construction of the house was not done properly there may not be an easy way to fix the problem. If the house is essentially a shack that was thrown together, there may not be any way to salvage it that will provide you with a profit. In a case like this it would probably be best to move on to the next prospect.

Condition

Is the house in repairable condition? It could be that a house is functionally obsolete. In this case no amount of rehab will be able to bring the house up to today's standards. This is especially true of very old homes. An older house may have rooms that are poorly laid out, inadequate plumbing or electrical systems and a host of other problems that could make complete demolition the most viable option.

When evaluating the condition you should start with the exterior. What is the condition of the roof? If it is in poor condition it should be replaced, trying to sell a house with a bad roof can be difficult at best. If there are chimneys, are they in decent shape? Is the siding in good condition or will it need to be repaired or replaced? How much landscaping work is required?

On the inside you should start with the various systems. Is the furnace in good shape or does it need to be replaced? This can be a big-ticket item so you should have it checked out if there is any doubt. If there are air conditioning units they should be checked as well. How old is the water heater? If it is near the end of its useful life you should plan on installing a new one. Pay close attention to the plumbing and electric, they have to be functioning properly. These are all items that a buyer will expect to be in good shape before they will buy a house. If you spend money in this area it won't have the "wow" factor of a new kitchen or bath but it has to be done if it is needed.

Most rehab projects are going to require that you update, if not totally replace, the kitchen and bathroom. What you should be on the lookout for are things that could be a major problem such as mold. Will the current layout allow for an easy renovation or will you need to make major changes?

Is the house in such poor condition that you should just gut it and start over? This is not necessarily a bad thing, it gives you a clean slate to work with and you can be more creative. If you plan on moving walls or windows you need to be careful, some walls are load-bearing. If you do plan to alter a load bearing wall you need to be sure that the structure is properly reinforced or you could wind up with a building collapse.

When evaluating a property, I always assume that the carpets will be replaced. If I encounter a situation where they can just be cleaned I consider that a bonus. I always plan on refinishing wood floors as well, if they don't need it, that's another plus. Paint is something that I always do, it gives the finished project a fresh, clean look.

Within Your Ability

Is the project within your ability? That doesn't mean that you need to be swinging the hammer yourself, it is perfectly reasonable to use contractors. However, it is important that you have an understanding of what is involved. If you aren't doing the work yourself you will still need to control the project. It is ultimately your responsibility to be sure that things go according to plan. There will always be surprises that pop up; it's part of the process. Effective management of the project plays a major role in its' ultimate profitability.

One of the major reasons that potential rehabbers fail is that they get in over their head. What seems like a small rehab project can be overwhelming to someone who has never done one. Even experienced rehabbers are prone to biting off more than they can chew occasionally. It is best to start small and graduate to larger projects as you gain experience.

Real Estate Terminology

When hunting for real estate you will come across certain terminology and abbreviations. Things like NOI, ROI, Cap Rate, GRM, Cash Flow and PITI to name a few. It is helpful to have a basic understanding of what these terms mean and their significance. Some terms pertain to residential rental houses and others to apartment buildings or commercial properties. We'll examine each of them briefly.

PITI

PITI is an abbreviation for *principal + interest + taxes + insurance*. You will usually see this used to represent the total payment for a house with a certain amount down. For example, you might see an advertisement that says $1200 per month PITI with 10% down. You will see real estate agents using this in advertisements for residential housing. It is designed to give you an idea of what your payment might be if you purchased it. This is not a guaranteed amount; the agent is making many assumptions to arrive at this figure. The taxes are most likely accurate but your homeowner's insurance may cost more or less than the assumed payment. The principal and interest payment depends on the actual terms of the loan, if you use the exact loan that the agent is showing then you can expect the numbers to be accurate but you will probably be using one with terms that are different than the ones being shown. The idea of showing the payment is to give you a ballpark idea of what you will be paying.

PITI can also be used when you are talking about an actual property with a loan already in place. If you are talking about your own payment and say that it is $1200 PITI then you are stating what your actual housing payment is, not a hypothetical payment.

NOI

NOI stands for *net operating income*. NOI can apply to any type of income property, residential or commercial. It is a fairly easy number to calculate. You take the total income and subtract all of the expenses including a vacancy factor and you are left with the net operating income or NOI. This number is calculated without any consideration given to mortgage or debt service. While the number is easy to calculate, it is very often misstated. In an effort to get a higher sale price you will often find that the income is overstated and expenses are minimized. That is why it is important to look at actual expenses and not assumptions.

Cash Flow

Cash flow is determined by subtracting the mortgage payments from the NOI. You will often see and hear statements like "positive cash flow" or "this property cash flows," take those statements with a grain of salt. Real estate agents will frequently say that a property has positive cash flow if the rent will cover the PITI and sometimes a small vacancy allowance. To determine if a property truly has a positive cash flow you need to look at all of the expenses and include a vacancy factor that is realistic for the market that the property is in. If the NOI is enough to cover the total mortgage payment then you have a positive cash flow. It is not that the agents are intentionally trying to be deceptive, but this is what they have been taught and most of them have never owned an investment property. That's why it is important to do your homework and calculate the expenses based on verifiable data.

Cap Rate

The Cap Rate, or *capitalization rate*, is a calculation used to help determine the value of a similar property. To calculate the cap rate you would take the value of a property and divide it by the NOI of the property. If a property is appraised at $300,000 and has an NOI of $30,000 annually, it would have a cap rate of 10 ($300,000/30,000 = 10). If you know the average cap rate for similar properties in the area you can determine how much a property is worth. If an area has an average of 8 and you are looking at a property with an NOI of $50,000 then you can determine that the fair market value of the property is $625,000.

Cap Rate = 8

NOI = $50,000

$50,000 / 8 = $625,000

This is just a starting point. You would need to evaluate the property to see if the condition is better or worse than average and if there are any major maintenance issues. The Cap Rate can help you spot potential deals and rule out overpriced properties. If you find a property that looks like a deal then you should investigate further to determine if all of the information is accurate. The Cap Rate has an inverse relationship to value. If the Cap Rate is a higher number than average then the property is undervalued and therefore a better deal. The higher the number the better the potential deal.

GRM

GRM is an abbreviation for gross rent multiplier and is similar in function to the Cap Rate. It is used primarily to evaluate apartment buildings. The main difference is that instead of using NOI you would use the gross rents. When using the GRM method you again use the average GRM for similar buildings in the area. The lower the GRM the better the property is as an investment.

GRM = Sale Price/Monthly Income

Market Value = GRM x Gross Income

ROI

One of the more important terms to any investor is ROI or *return on investment*. It is simply the rate of return on money that you have invested. If you put $100 in the bank and earn $5 in interest in a year you have a 5% return on investment. Your investment is the $100 deposit and the return is the $5 in interest that you earned. Real estate is a little different because of the use of leverage. If you buy a house for $100,000 using cash for the purchase and the house appreciates to $105,000 in a year, you have a $5,000 return or 5%. However people rarely use cash, they use a mortgage or leverage to make the purchase. If you buy that same house for $100,000 and it appreciates to $105,000 in a year you have still made $5,000. But if you only put down $10,000 and obtained a mortgage for the difference your rate of return is not the same. You made $5,000 but only invested $10,000 so your return on investment is actually 50%. This is why so many people like investing in real estate.

There are many more terms used in real estate but these are the most common ones that you will come across when searching for property. While you may never use some of them, it is good to have an understanding of what the terms mean.

Summary

Evaluate:

- Structure
- Condition
- Your Ability to Complete the Project

Learn Terminology:

- PITI

- NOI

- Cash Flow

- Cap Rate

- GRM

- ROI

A Rehabber's Tale
Ely, Ave B

One of the best ways to get a great deal is to buy from a distressed landlord. Many people buy rental properties with the idea of creating wealth but soon find that the reality of being a landlord does not suit them. They wind up reaching a point of frustration where the only thing that they care about is getting rid of the property and, with it, the headaches. The last thing that a distressed landlord is concerned with is the profit, they just want out.

I found just this kind of deal in Ely, Nevada. A former resident of the area who had moved to another state owned the house. The market was not good at the time that they moved so they rented it out. The tenant was not diligent about paying his rent on time and had a very cavalier attitude about it. The owner did use a property manager but they were not able to do much. It seems that the tenant paid the rent when he felt like it and knew exactly when to pay to avoid eviction.

The adjacent house, which was a little larger and a lot nicer, had just sold for as little over $100,000. This house was listed at $45,000. It was a good deal at that price but I made an offer of $35,000 subject to an inspection report and obtaining financing. The seller looked to split the difference and countered at $40,000. I agreed to $40,000 if the seller would contribute $2,000 towards my closing costs, they agreed to pay $1500 and we had a deal.

The exterior of this house was in excellent condition but the interior needed a lot of work. I applied for a mortgage, which was approved with 10% down. It cost me a total of $5,000 out-of-pocket to buy the house and I had a mortgage of $36,000. I now owned the house but I also inherited the problem tenant. The property manager sent a very strongly worded letter in regards to timely payment of rent. He complied for the first two months but was late the third month. I had expected this.

When the rent was late I had the property manager send him a 30-day notice that the rent was being increased from $450 per month to

$575, which was what similar houses in the area were renting for. I was able to do this because he was on a month-to-month lease. He promptly moved out rather than pay the increase. The former owner could have solved the tenant problem by simply raising the rent. I now had gotten rid of the problem and I could begin rehabbing the house.

The interior was in need of a lot of work. The entire house needed to be painted and the carpets needed to be replaced. The vinyl flooring in the kitchen was in such poor condition that new underlayment had to be put down before the floor could be installed. The stove was also replaced and the refrigerator needed a good cleaning. The bathroom needed a new toilet as well as repairs to the shower. The exterior of the house was in good shape but some landscaping work was needed. When all was said and done, I spent about $4,000 getting it ready for the next tenant.

The house was rented fairly quickly for $575 per month. Recent BPOs, or broker price opinions, have placed the current value at about $95,000. I have doubled my money in a little over a year. After all expenses are paid including the mortgage and a reserve for maintenance I have a slightly positive cash flow. I will probably hold onto this property for a while since the area has been experiencing very strong appreciation with the potential for a lot more.

Chapter 5

Finding a Property

Opportunity is missed by most people because it is dressed in overalls and looks like work.
—Thomas A. Edison

So where do you find these properties? Finding the right deal can be the hardest part. Finding houses that need work is easy; finding those houses at a price that can produce a profit is extremely difficult. What is needed is a motivated seller. Many sellers say they are motivated but what they usually mean is that they are willing to sell slightly below market. That is not good enough. If it were easy to find deals everyone would be doing it and making tons of money in the process. It is very much a numbers game; you look at enough properties from a number of different sources and you eventually find one that meets your criteria, but where do you look?

Real Estate Agents

Your first instinct might be to work with a real estate agent and utilize the Multiple Listing Service or MLS. The truth is that very few agents have any real knowledge of rehab. This definitely rules out your

Uncle Floyd, the barber who happens to have a real estate license. They may have some very basic knowledge and talk a good game, but unless they have rehab experience themselves they probably don't know any more than you do. On the other hand, a real estate agent that truly does know this aspect of the business can be worth their weight in gold. These agents are probably rehabbers themselves and can keep you from making many mistakes. The main thing to keep in mind when working with any agent is that they get paid to sell houses; if they don't make sales, they can't feed their families. Due to the very nature of the way they are paid, agents will usually tend to look at the bright side of things and spin market information in a favorable way. They may not be intentionally trying to mislead anyone but could you imagine them saying that "the sky is falling" even if it really is? They wouldn't make many sales that way.

If you are going to work with a real estate agent, what do you look for? You need to set criteria ahead of time, letting the agent know what you are looking for in terms of the amount of work a house needs and your price range. When using the MLS, you may look for tell-tale signs such as price reductions, days on the market and a price per square foot that is significantly lower than similar houses. If the number of days on the market is significantly higher than average, that could be an indication that the house has problems. A price reduction could mean that the seller is ready to deal. A lower price per square foot ratio could also indicate that the house needs work. Do not forget that you are looking for a truly motivated seller who absolutely needs to sell now. The important thing to remember is that you need to stick to your criteria and not be swayed by an agent's overly optimistic take on things. One other thing to avoid is having an agent handle both sides of a transaction. An agent who represents both the buyer and the seller cannot possibly be truly objective. It is usually better to have the buyer and seller represented by different agents.

FSBO

Many homeowners elect to sell their property without using an agent; these properties are considered FSBOs, or For Sale By Owner. There can be many opportunities here. When a property owner sells a property without an agent, he must handle advertising, show the property and handle all negotiations. The owner is looking to save the bulk of the listing fee this way. The buyer would expect to purchase the home at a lower price as well.

I have found that houses listed as FSBO fall into two broad categories: The first is the one listed by an owner who wants to keep the money that is normally paid to an agent. He figures that selling a home isn't all that hard, just put an ad in the paper and a sign on the lawn. It is hard to get a good deal from this type of seller at first. If the home remains unsold for any length of time the owner may come to realize that selling a house is not as easy as he thought and he might be more willing to make a deal at that point.

The second type of FSBO is where you can find a great deal. Imagine a homeowner who is looking to sell a house through traditional means. He interviews several agents and selects one that he believes will bring him the best price for his property. The house is listed, placed on the MLS, advertised, and the agent schedules an open house. Many potential buyers come through but there are no offers. Perhaps the agent was so eager to get the listing that he convinced the buyer that he could get a higher price than was realistic for the market. After several months without any activity the listing expires. The seller comes to the conclusion that the agent did not know what he was doing so he signs with a different agent and drops the price. In the meantime the market has softened and prices have fallen even further. The end result is that there is no activity with the new agent. It is now eight or nine months without a sale and the seller is getting desperate, he has to move.

The next step for this seller when the listing expires is to try to sell it himself. He figures that he can drop the price by the amount that he would have given to the agent. He is feeling the pressure to find a buyer and will accept any offer that will get him out of the house. This is the point at which you can make a great deal and get concessions from the seller. When you see a house that becomes a FSBO after being listed for a while, be prepared, opportunity may be about to knock.

Bird Dogs

Another way to find potential projects is to use property locators also known as Bird Dogs. Just as hunters will use bird dogs to flush their quarry out of the brush, you can use the real estate version of the bird dog to help you find your next house. A bird dog can be a full-time scout or just someone who happens to spot a possible deal. A professional bird dog will spend a lot of time seeking out deals and passing them on to investors in exchange for a finders-fee. The size of the fee varies based on the involvement of the person who locates the property and the deal you have with them. One investor may not be interested in a particular property but will pass it on to another who may be. In that case the fee could be a simple thank you or a small cash payment depending on the investor's relationship with each other. In other cases the fee could range from a few hundred to several thousand dollars depending on the quality of the deal. Since the bird dog does not assume any risk they generally will not earn a substantial fee. They will usually spot a possible deal and make a few inquiries as to the situation and if the house could be for sale, they will also get a general idea of what might be needed in the way of repairs. The better the quality of the information, the higher the fee that they can be expect.

Wholesaler

A wholesaler is another great source of property. A wholesaler will actually place a property under contract and then assign the contract to an investor without ever taking ownership. Wholesalers find property in a number of different ways including advertising. They may place ads that say, "We buy houses" indicating that they will accept any condition and close fast. They will generally be looking for people who absolutely must sell and do not have the time to wait for a house to be sold in the usual manner. They are also purchasing the properties at a deep discount, or wholesale, and then offering the house to an investor and receiving an assignment fee. The fee will be set by the wholesaler but cannot be so high as to make the price of the property unattractive to an investor. Fees can range from 1%–5% depending on the price of the property and how much of a discount the wholesaler was able to get on the property.

Why would a homeowner sell at a steep discount? They may not have a choice. Foreclosure could be looming or there could be a court ordered sale and they must close quickly. Some people are just tired of the property and want to unload it at any price. Or the property could be in such poor condition that no normal buyer would consider it. When the cost of selling the property through traditional means is considered, the wholesalers' price might not seem so unattractive to the seller.

Consider the following example:
Property valued at $100,000

Mortgage Payment	$600/month
Taxes	100/month
Insurance	50/month
Utilities	150/month
Miscellaneous Expenses	100/month
Total Expenses =	1,000/month
Real Estate Commission @ 6%	*$6,000*
Closing Costs @ 2%	*2,000*
Cost to sell	*$8,000*

If it takes 6 months from the listing date to the sale close the buyer will incur $6,000 of out-of-pocket costs, and selling costs of $8,000, for a total of $14,000. This means that the seller will net $86,000 on the sale but must also wait six months for everything to be done. If the seller is facing a hardship or simply has to sell now, a wholesaler's offer of $70,000 might not seem unreasonable. That price is just being used as an example and a wholesaler will only make an offer based on what he will be able to resell the property for given the condition of the house and the state of the local market.

Sale Price	100,000
Cost to Sell	(8,000)
Holding Expense x 6	(6,000)
Net Sale	86,000

A wholesaler must be careful because they are taking a risk by actually placing a house under contract. If they are not able to assign the contract to an investor or get out of the contract they will have to go through with the purchase or forfeit any earnest money that they deposited. They will protect themselves by putting several different clauses in the purchase contract. The most important being "and/or assigns" after their name. This allows them to assign the contract to someone else. Other clauses can be "subject to" or "contingent upon" things such as a "favorable appraisal" or an "inspection acceptable to the buyer" or obtaining financing. These clauses are deliberately vague and allow them to back out of a contract if they need to.

Foreclosures

Foreclosures are another way to obtain property. When a borrower defaults on a home loan, or mortgage, the lender begins the process of foreclosing on the property. The process varies from state to state depending on the laws in place. A late payment will generate a late notice to the borrower and after a certain period of time the lender will file a "notice of default" and begin the process of taking back the property. These notices are public record and can be viewed by anyone. There are companies in existence that watch for these notices to be filed and then sell lists of defaulting borrowers to interested parties. While you can obtain this information yourself, many people find it easier to purchase the lists. This period of time is often referred to as *pre-foreclosure* because it precedes the actual foreclosure sale.

The pre-foreclosure period can be an excellent time to get a good deal on a property. The owner is obviously having financial difficulty and is likely to be motivated to sell the property and avoid having the stigma of a foreclosure appear on his credit report. This is a time when the owner will sell at any possible price just to unload the house. One thing to keep in mind, however, is the mental state of the owner. Many homeowners are in complete denial at this stage and refuse to believe that the foreclosure will actually happen.

Not only is this a good time to make a deal, it is even possible to purchase the property for less than is owed through a *short sale*. A short sale must be approved by the lender and is usually only considered when the property is worth less than the amount that is owed. The lender has no desire to own the property and will incur significant expenses in the foreclosure and sale process. Rather than go through that process, the lender may agree to accept less than the balance that is remaining on the loan.

In today's market, it is quite common for homeowners to be upside down on their mortgage. Being upside down means that the home is worth less than the remaining balance of the mortgage. The proliferation of creative mortgage products and the relaxing of down payment standards encouraged people to purchase houses that they couldn't really afford. Many buyers were enticed into using adjustable rate loans, or ARMs, and payment option ARMs that allowed payments with negative amortization. Negative amortization means that the payment was not sufficient to pay the interest due and the excess interest was added to the principal balance of the loan. The theory was that the house was appreciating so it didn't matter if the mortgage balance grew. The adjustable rate loans looked good initially because the payments were lower in the beginning of the loan. At some point the interest rate would increase, or adjust, causing the payments to go up. If the borrower's income didn't increase, he would have trouble meeting the monthly payments and wind up defaulting on the loan.

The combination of adjustable rate mortgages, low down or no down payment loans, reduced or no documentation requirements and rising interest rates have led to a dramatic increase in the default rate on mortgages. This, in turn, has created a huge number of desperate sellers who want nothing more than to get rid of their property.

The thing to remember is that just because a seller is truly motivated doesn't mean that you can get a good deal. If the seller owes more than the house is worth and you are unable to negotiate a favorable short sale, then you need to move on to the next potential deal.

The property can also be purchased at the actual foreclosure sale. When the borrower is unable to sell the home prior to the foreclosure date the house is placed up for auction. This proceeding typically takes place on the county courthouse steps. Quite often this is merely a formality and the only bidder is the lender who then places a bid equal to the amount owed and takes possession of the property. It is not easy to purchase a house at the auction because you have to have funds available in the amount of the bid and be prepared to take possession immediately and accept the property "as-is" without having had a chance to inspect the property. However it is possible to make a good deal in this manner if the property has a substantial amount of equity.

REO

After a property is taken back by the lender it is placed in its *REO* portfolio, REO is an abbreviation for Real Estate Owned. The lender's REO division will evaluate the property and assign it to a Real Estate Agency for sale. In the past, these properties were generally priced very near market value and would not usually be considered a bargain. The recent increase in the foreclosure rate has created huge REO portfolios at many banks. The banks do not want this real estate on their balance sheets and need to move it. One of the difficulties, however, is that these portfolios are managed by hourly employees who are not highly motivated to complete any particular deal. This can lead to frustration for the investor. When dealing with banks and their REOs you need to be patient. You may make an offer on a property today that a bank turns down but would be willing to accept after the property has been sitting for several months. The key point to remember is that, just like any other deal, you need to do your homework. While it may take some work to uncover a true gem, it could be well worth it.

HUD/VA

Government agencies also deal in foreclosed homes. Many people acquire homes through the use of loans issued through programs of the Veterans Administration (VA) and the United States Department of Housing and Urban Development's Federal Housing Administration (FHA). When these homes go through the foreclosure process they wind up with HUD and the VA who then sell them through a sealed bid process. The easiest way to obtain information on these homes is through the government website at www.homesles.gov. These homes are also handled by real estate agents working with the government agencies. Information on the bidding process can be obtained through the agency website. These homes are often available to owner-occupants only during the first round of bidding. If the homes remain unsold past a certain date investors are able to bid as well. Initially these homes are listed near their market value, if they remain unsold the price will be lowered and lower bids may be considered. Another positive feature of this process is that there is usually a property condition report, which gives you an idea of what might be wrong with the property. This report is not intended to be a replacement for your own inspection.

Some of the HUD and VA homes are eligible for financing. Others are not in good enough condition for financing to be available. When bidding for the homes you need to put up an earnest money deposit. The money is refundable in some circumstances but can be forfeited if you back out of the deal. The deposit amounts are small and in some cases it may be better to walk away and forfeit the deposit than to complete the deal if you find that you have made a major mistake.

Advertising

Many rehabbers will advertise in much the same way those wholesalers do. They will place ads in newspapers and low cost publications saying things like "We buy houses, any condition, all cash, fast close." They also use bandit signs, which are small signs you see on the side of the road or posted in many other places. They can be very simple and say something like "We Buy Houses," or they may add things like "any condition," "all cash," "fast close," or other terms to attract someone who is desperate. Bandit signs are inexpensive but you can expect to go through a lot of them. You might find them disappearing almost as fast as you put them up. You also should be aware of local ordinances that may prohibit their use in certain locations.

Estate Sales

Estate sales can be another good way to acquire a property. When someone dies and the property needs to be sold in order to distribute money to the heirs it is possible to make a favorable deal. Sometimes the heirs will insist on getting market value or close to it, but other times the heirs just want the executor of the estate to dispose of the property quickly. Multiple heirs can be both a blessing and a curse. If several people are going to inherit the property but are unable to agree on the price or terms you can have an ugly situation on your hands. On the other hand, if the primary motivation is to sell quickly so that they can get their money, they may be more willing to deal. If you have 5 heirs and ask them to cut the price by $25,000 that is only $5,000 each. They may figure that giving up $5,000 is acceptable if it results in a quick transaction.

Auctions

One method that is becoming more popular is the use of auctions to sell homes. Prior to attempting to use this method you need to understand the process. An auction can be an absolute auction or a reserve auction. In an absolute auction the house will be sold to the highest bidder regardless of price. There may be a starting price or minimum bid but once the auction starts the property is awarded to the bidder with the highest price. Another type of auction is a reserve auction. In this type of auction the seller can set a reserve price or minimum price that he will accept. This reserve price will be higher than the starting price. If the winning bid is less than the reserve price the seller has the option of keeping the property. The idea of using the reserve price is that the starting price can be set low enough to attract interest to the auction. The seller hopes that the bidding action will drive the price over the reserve price that has been set. If you are going to participate in an auction be sure to understand all of the rules. What are the payment terms? Is there a provision to have the property inspected? Under what conditions can you void the deal? Be sure that you understand all of these things prior to submitting a bid.

Tax Liens

Some states also sell *tax liens.* When a homeowner does not pay the taxes on a home the municipality will place a lien on the property for the amount owed. These tax liens may be sold to investors. The homeowner has the right to clear the lien by paying the back taxes, interest and any penalties that are due. If they do not pay the lien holder has the right to foreclose on the property. Each state has different laws regarding the tax lien procedure and the rights of the homeowner to pay what is owed and have the lien removed. If the amount owed is paid the investor who purchased the lien will receive his initial investment back along with any interest he is entitled to. Since the laws vary from state to state you would need to check with them to see what the procedures are and how long the delinquent homeowner has to repay the amount owed. Most liens will not go into foreclosure so there is no guarantee that you can obtain a house in this manner.

Networking

One of the best ways to find suitable property is through *networking.* The more people who are aware of what you are looking for the more likely you are to have someone tell you about a potential deal. You should have business cards made with your contact information and a summary of what you are looking for. You never know where your next deal will come from but if people aren't aware that you are looking they will not think to contact you if they come across something.

Networking can be formal as well as informal. An informal setting can be casual conversation at a party, barbecue or other social gathering. When appropriate, you can let people know what you are looking for. A formal event can be business mixers where other business people gather to exchange information and make new contacts. The local Chamber of Commerce or other business group may sponsor these events. There are also networking groups that meet on a regular basis for breakfast or lunch for the purpose of exchanging leads and other information. Many of these groups will allow you to come as a guest prior to making a decision on whether or not to join.

The whole idea of networking, either formally or informally, is to expand your circle of contacts. The more people who know you the better the odds of finding something before others do. You will also find that networking is helpful when you need the services of others. It is always better to utilize someone with whom you have established a relationship that it is to deal with strangers.

You should network with other investors as well as real estate agents, mortgage brokers, title and escrow officers. While investors may be competing for the same properties in some cases, they can also be a great resource. Being in contact with other investors can be invaluable when it comes to dealing with problems. Who better to ask for advice than someone who has been in a similar situation? You may actually find yourself teaming up with other investors on projects or on locating suitable deals.

A great place to meet other people in the business is by joining a local *real estate investment club*. These clubs meet on a regular basis, usually monthly, to offer educational and networking opportunities to members. The topics can cover a wide variety of real estate related areas and be a great way to expand you knowledge. Many clubs will have sponsors who pay to be able to offer their products or services to the club members. While that portion of the meeting is a sales pitch, it also gives you the opportunity to hear about other things that are available. However, the best part about belonging to a club is the contacts that you will make who can assist you with your real estate ventures.

Another good way to find deals is to pursue your interests but be sure that everyone knows what you are looking for. Whatever your hobbies and interests are can work for you. Have a ready supply of business cards with your contact information. Don't waste the back of the card by keeping it blank, this is a great spot to list what you are looking for. You may have a line on the front that says "We Buy Houses" and a listing on the back of the types of houses that you are looking for. Whenever you get someone else's card look it over in order to get ideas for your own cards. These cards should be with you at all times and you should hand them out at every opportunity. Business cards can be the cheapest form of advertising that you do.

As you can see, there are so many ways to find out about deals that may be available. The best thing to do is to try a little bit of everything and find out what works best for you. There is not necessarily a right way or a wrong way; you just need to find your way. Happy hunting!

Summary

Locating Properties:

- Real Estate Agents

- FSBO

- Bird Dog

- Wholesaler

- Foreclosures

- REO

- HUD/VA

- Advertising

- Estate Sales

- Auctions

- Tax Liens

- Networking

A Rehabber's Tale

Tony

Tony was a new real estate investor who was interested in rehabbing his first property. He spent time educating himself and preparing to make his first purchase. He looked at a number of different houses in the Ely area and found one that seemed suitable. The problem was that he had never rehabbed a property before and was not sure where to begin. Prior to purchasing the home he had me look it over with him to determine the needs. I agreed with him that it was a viable deal and was well worth pursuing.

In evaluating the house we determined that it would need a new roof including removing the existing shingles and making repairs to the roof deck. The house needed to be completely repainted and the carpets needed to be cleaned. The bathroom was in such poor shape that the only solution was to completely gut it and start over. The kitchen needed some work but did not require an extensive makeover. The landscaping was out of control and needed to be taken care of as well. All told, we determined that the scope of work should allow for a reasonable profit.

While going through the negotiation process with the seller, Tony came to the conclusion that this was not a project that he could tackle himself and he asked me if I would be willing to be his partner on the deal. I agreed and we decided that Tony would make the purchase and I would handle all aspects of the rehab. We had a formal agreement in which Tony would handle all costs related to the purchase and ownership of the house and that I would fund the rehab portion. In the end we would both be reimbursed for all expenditures and then we would split the profits. Tony purchased the house for $55,000 using conventional financing. There were some issues with the roof which made it difficult to get the loan approved but it was all eventually worked out.

After closing escrow it was time to go to work. With winter fast approaching the roof was the number one priority. Most people think of Nevada as being a hot, dry desert, but northern Nevada is very different. Ely has an elevation of 6500 feet, which makes it very cold in winter with a fair amount of snow. I knew that we didn't have long to get the job done. The old roof had been done in stages over the years and was like a patchwork quilt. Some areas were in good shape while others were in extremely poor condition. In addition to tearing off the old roof, many repairs to the roof deck were needed. This slowed down the process and each day seemed to be colder and darker. The roofing project was completed just in time and it was actually snowing as I capped off the final section.

Once the roof was completed, it was on to the inside. The next priority was the bathroom. There had been several leaks which, in time, had rotted away sections of the subfloor. The only solution was to remove all of the flooring and start over. Since the bathroom was being completely redone I was able to alter the layout so that it was a much better floor plan. By moving the doorway to one side instead of having it centered, I was able to have a better placement of the fixtures. I installed a new tub, toilet, sink and vanity. I added a medicine cabinet with mirror, new lighting and a ceiling light with built-in exhaust fan. In the end the house had a modern bathroom that would show well at the time of sale.

The kitchen was fairly easy to complete. The old cabinets were in good shape and just needed to be painted. The stove didn't work but I was able to purchase a floor model at a very reasonable cost. I added a fresh coat of paint and some updated lighting and that portion was complete. The vinyl flooring had some bad spots but we were able to avoid a total replacement. While the kitchen was not a masterpiece, it was on par with other houses in the area.

While I was working on the roof, I had a cleanup man come in to work on the yard. He was a local handyman who would do just about any kind of job. He removed all of the junk that was in the yard and trimmed the bushes. He removed some overgrown shrubs and trimmed the trees. All together he worked about a day and a half and charged $250 for the work, a real bargain. When he was done it looked like a totally different house. Had the previous owner done this work prior to listing the house for sale he would have been able to command a better price. The little things really do matter.

Back inside I painted the walls and ceiling and had the carpets cleaned. There were a lot of little things that needed to be done and it took several days to complete the tasks. The house was now ready for sale. The real estate agent suggested a listing price of $105,000, but we settled on $99,900 in the hope of making a quick sale. We found a buyer very quickly and negotiated a price of $95,000. When the dust settled Tony and I wound up splitting a profit of just under $24,000 after all expenses. It was not a homerun type of deal but it was a reasonable profit and an invaluable learning experience for Tony. Tony has since gone on to do other deals using the knowledge that he gained on his first one.

Chapter 6

Is it a Good Deal?

*A once in a lifetime opportunity comes along
about once a week; you just need to recognize it,
be open to it and, if appropriate, act on it.*
—**Frank Warren**

One of the main reasons that people lose money when trying to rehab
a house is that they pay too much for it. Most people do not know how
to evaluate a house in terms of potential profit. Sadly, this generaliza-
tion would include the majority of real estate agents. That is not to say
that they are trying to steer you into a bad deal, it's just that they do not
have the experience required to know what truly is a good deal. There
are just so many unexpected costs involved with rehab projects that
can turn what seems like a good deal into a loser.

I have actually read articles by real estate agents, and others claiming to be gurus when it comes to rehab, who tout buying properties at
15–20% below market. That just shows that they do not really know
anything about rehabbing houses. If you were to buy a property for
rehab at 20% below market, you would be almost guaranteed to lose

money. There are too many costs involved and too many unknowns that must be accounted for.

Is This a Deal?

Let's try an example. Suppose we were to purchase a house with a market value of $250,000 for $200,000, which is 20% below market. Let's also assume that it only needs $20,000 in repairs. It looks like we have a potential profit of $30,000, not bad. In fact, this is similar to the scenarios shown in a lot of the house flipping shows on TV.

Now let's take it a step further. We'll assume that the project will take a total of 4 months from purchase until the sale is final. In that time we are going to have some routine carrying costs. These costs include things like insurance, taxes, utilities and other everyday expenses. For the sake of argument we will assume that these are only about $250 per month for a total of $1,000. This takes the potential profit down to $29,000. Still not a bad deal.

But what about financing? If you have the cash in hand, your financing cost is only the amount that you could have earned on your money if it was invested elsewhere. It is more likely that you are going to have to borrow the money. Getting a loan for a rehab project is not the same as getting a home mortgage from a bank. A mortgage lender does not want to loan on a house that is in need of a significant amount of repair. This means that you will have to deal with lenders who specialize in loans for distressed properties. These are known as Hard Money Lenders. These lenders will typically loan money based on the after repaired value (ARV) of the home and can include the cost of repairs itself. The maximum loan amounts are usually 60–70% of ARV. The terms are generally steep and include a high rate of interest as well as points. A point is equal to 1% of the amount borrowed. The number of points varies and will be lower for people who have done a number of deals with the lender. These points can range from 3–7% of the loan amount.

Let's get back to our example. We'll assume we can get a loan for 70% of ARV which amounts to $175,000. We'll assume that we are paying 4 points or $7,000. At 18% interest that amounts to 1.5% per month for 4 months or $10,500.

$250,000   = ARV

x 70%

175,000   = Loan Amount

175,000

x 4%

  7,000   = Points

175,000

x 1.5%

x4

 10,500   = Interest

$17,500   = Finance Cost

Now we subtract our finance cost from our profit, $29,000 - 17,500, and we are left with a profit of $11,500. While this is not as good as it first looked, we still have a profit.

In this scenario you will also need to come up with cash for the purchase, repairs and carrying costs. In many cases the financing costs will not need to be paid until the sale closes. So if we buy for $200,000 and have carrying costs of $1,000 and repairs of $20,000, we have a total of $221,000 ($200,000 + 1,000 + 20,000 = 221,000). Since you could only borrow $175,000, that means that you must come up with $46,000 ($221,000 - 175,000 = 46,000). If you do not have this money available you will not be able to do the project. If you do have it, your money is tied up until the sale closes.

Oops! What about selling? Let's return to our scenario. We'll assume that you would be able to sell at market value (if the market is slow you may not be able to.) When selling, you have other costs to consider, such as real estate commission, title charges, transfer taxes and any other costs associated with the sale. A typical real estate commission is 6% and we will use 2% as a total for the other costs in this example. If the sale price is indeed $250,000 you will have commission of $15,000 and other selling expenses of $5,000 for a total of $20,000. This will give us a net sale of $230,000 ($250,000 - 20,000 = 230,000).

So how did we do? Let's see:

$250,000	Sale Price
(200,000)	Purchase Price
(15,000)	Commission
(5,000)	Selling Expense
(17,500)	Finance Cost
(1,000)	Carrying Cost
(20,000)	Rehab Cost
(8,500)	**Profit/(Loss)**

Apparently we did not do so well! We tied up our cash and took a large amount of risk in order to lose $8,500. This is also making the assumption that we did not go over the repair budget or time estimate and that we were able to sell quickly. The reality is that you will often go over the budget and it will frequently take longer than you expect. Selling quickly is also not a sure thing, even if you price it right. The market could slow down or it could be holiday season. You could also have buyers who are denied a mortgage or back out of a deal. Every day that the house sits on the market, a little more of your profit gets eaten away or your loss grows.

Unfortunately the preceding example is typical of what happens when people try to rehab houses without first educating themselves about the process. Many people are encouraged to get into bad deals by real estate agents trying to make a sale. It's not that they are trying to hurt people; they truly believe that buying a house for 15–20% below market is a good deal. I have often seen real estate agents, who portray themselves as savvy and investment oriented, touting homes as good rehab candidates when there is little possibility of making a profit. This is especially evident in a slow market when agents are trying all sorts of creative ways to make sales and feed their families. As you gain more knowledge of rehabbing you will be able to quickly tell the true experts from those that are just pretending.

Why do people get involved in deals like this if they cannot make a profit? The main reason is that they do not do their homework. Buying a $250,000 house for $200,000 sounds like a great deal. If they would take the time to truly figure out what their total costs will be, then they would never do it. Unfortunately many people jump in without getting the facts; they see the house flipping TV shows and think it's easy to make a lot of money. The whole trick to the rehab game is to know when you have a good deal and knowing when to walk away and keep looking.

A Better Way

So how do you know? There will always be risk involved, but you can minimize it by sticking to some very simple rules:

- Accurately estimate the market value after repair (ARV).
- Carefully estimate the renovation cost.
- Figure out the time needed to complete the project.

- Determine how long it will take to sell.
- Allow for the unexpected.

Let's break these down one by one.

Determine the ARV

How do you determine the After Repair Value or ARV? You arrive at this figure by looking at comparables, much as you would with any other property you were considering. You assume that the house has been repaired to the area standard. You need to be careful about investing more in renovations than you can get back when you sell. There is a fine line here, if your house is better than others in the neighborhood it will be easier to sell. But, if you put so much into the renovations that the house is significantly better than the rest of the neighborhood you will have a hard time recouping the additional money spent. If the house still isn't up to par with other houses in the area when you are finished, people are going to expect that the price will be discounted. Without a doubt, this is a balancing act. A lot of it depends upon how weak or strong the real estate market is in the area. If the market is very strong you can get away with less. Conversely, if the market is weak you may need to do more to attract buyers.

After you have figured out the standard for the area you need to research comparable sales. The more active the market the easier it will be to do this. If you have a good real estate agent that you work with they will be able to do this for you. However you need to keep in mind the words of Ronald Reagan, "Trust, but verify." Always double-check the information that you are given. If you tend to work in the same area you will come to know the value of houses. You can also use various Web sites that provide house values, just remember that the information is not always accurate. Another way to get the same information is to search the county records for recent sales in the area. The one thing you need to be sure of is that you are doing an "apples to apples" comparison. You also need to keep in mind that markets are always changing; the older the data the less reliable it is.

Estimate Repairs

The next step is to estimate the repairs needed and their cost. If you have extensive contracting experience this part should be easy. However, the vast majority of people do not. So if you don't have the experience what do you do? The number one thing that you need to do is to establish a relationship with a contractor that you can trust. This is easier said than done. Good contractors are usually busy and the thought of going around to look at houses with you is not something that they are likely to do. You will need to learn to do some basic estimating yourself. The idea is not to come up with exact figures, but to quickly figure out whether or not a house you are looking at is one that you should walk away from or one that you should check out further.

You can get some basic information from contractors. Explain to them what you are doing and ask them for the price range for a bathroom renovation or a kitchen makeover. You can get an idea of what it costs to replace a roof or have a house painted inside and out. These are just ballpark numbers to help you determine where to go next. As you look at a property you can see if the roof might need to be replaced or the bathroom and kitchen redone. Does it need paint? What about the plumbing, electric and foundation? If you walk through the house and add up what might be needed you may quickly figure out that the price is too high. If the price still seems to make sense, then it is time to call in the experts for accurate estimates. If you are unsure of something, have it checked out. As you do more rehabbing you will come to know what things are going to cost, that's just experience.

Time

Another area where people blow it is when estimating the amount of time needed. Rehabbers, by their very nature, are optimists. You need to be in order to look at the ugly duckling of the neighborhood and see a beautiful swan. This optimism is a double-edged sword. It can help you to envision the possibilities but also cause you to under-estimate the amount of time needed to complete a project. If you are working with contractors they can give you an estimate of how long a project will take, but you must understand that it may not be accurate. Contractors are infamous for taking longer than expected or not showing up at all. They may be working more than one job at a time and not giving you their undivided attention. There are also unexpected problems that arise as well as weather delays or delays in getting the needed materials. The TV programs that show a major project being completed in a week or two are pure fantasy. The bigger the project is the bigger the cushion you need to build into your time estimate.

Sale

Another factor in the time estimate is guessing how long it will take to sell. If you are in a strong market, and you price it right then selling the house shouldn't be a problem. If the market is not strong, or is actually slow, you will need to allow more time to sell and price the home below market. Every day that the house is on the market your profit is being eaten away. Pricing the house lower for a quick sale may actually net you more than putting it up for sale at the market price and waiting to sell. The problem that many people have is that they do not think about this until it is time to sell. This is something that should be addressed prior to making an offer to buy the house, if selling could be a problem you need to pay less when you buy.

A strong indicator of the market is the inventory of houses for sale and the days on market. Inventory alone does not tell the story. If the number of buyers is less than the number of houses coming on the market the days on market figure will grow. If there are more buyers than sellers the number will shrink. You need to consider historical numbers and seasonal trends as well. In many areas the number of homes on the market will increase in the spring but so will the number of people looking for homes. In most areas winter is a slow time and you need to evaluate those numbers differently. You also need to watch out for holiday seasons. Historically there are far fewer buyers between Thanksgiving and New Years Day. If you are going to rehab a property, you need to be aware of when you anticipate putting it on the market. If you place a property on the market in mid November you may not be able to sell it for months simply because of the time of year. On the other hand, if you time a project so the house comes on the market during a prime selling season, you may be able to sell quicker and for a higher price. The other thing to be aware of is that some unforeseen event could cause a market to come to a standstill leaving you with a property that is difficult to sell. When you estimate the ARV on a house, you are basing it on where you need to price it in order to sell in 30 days or less.

The Unexpected

This brings us to the last item, allowing for the unexpected. It is one thing to expect things to happen, but how do you allow for it? When working on an older property there are some things that occur from time to time. Things like plumbing or electrical problems, structural problems, termites or other infestation issues, water damage, mold and a host of other similar conditions. They may not be found during initial inspections but show up later as the work is being done. While you were not expecting to have these problems they are not unusual. It is rare to have a project where everything goes as expected unless, of course, you were expecting everything to go wrong. Since it is impossible to know exactly what will go wrong we need to make allowances for things that might go wrong.

What kind of allowances do you make? The easiest way to do it is to use a percentage of the total project budget for both money and time. Padding the budget by 10–15% should cover most of the minor things that could crop up. On an older house a larger reserve is in order due to the age of the property. In the case of an older home you may wish to use a cushion of 20–25%. In the case of a major renovation project where you know there will be problems you may want an even larger reserve. If you build in an allowance and nothing major comes up your project will be under budget and ahead of schedule. This is not a bad thing, having no allowance for the unexpected and encountering problems is a recipe for disaster.

While you never know what may crop up, you do know that things will. Try to avoid being overly optimistic by leaving too small of an allowance in order to justify a deal. If you find yourself fudging the numbers to convince yourself that you have a good deal on your hands then you should be prepared to get burned. The truth is that a deal either pencils out or it doesn't, don't try to force it. Whatever allowance you have deemed appropriate is added to your overall cost of repairs.

A Winning Formula

Now that you have gathered all of this information, you need to see if the house fits our winning formula. If you follow this formula closely you will rarely have a losing deal:

(After Repair Value X 70%) - Repair Cost = Maximum Price

Let's try that house again. If the house is worth $250,000 after repair and needs $20,000 worth of work how much should we pay?

($250,000 x 70%) - $20,000 = Maximum Price

$175,000 - 20,000 = $155,000

The most we should pay would be $155,000. Will it be easy to find a deal like that? Probably not, but it can be done. Buying at this price will greatly reduce the need to come out of pocket on the deal. We may need to contribute some cash but not the $46,000 needed in the first example.

Let's see how it works this time.

$250,000	Sale Price
(155,000)	Purchase Price
(15,000)	Commission
(5,000)	Selling Expense
(17,500)	Finance Cost
(1,000)	Carrying Cost
(20,000)	Rehab Cost
$36,500	**Profit/(Loss)**

A much better result!

The formula takes into account the cost of selling as well as using hard money. If you anticipate a longer hold due to the scope of work or market conditions you may need to adjust your formula. If you antici-pate a hold time that is longer than 4–5 months you should adjust the formula by reducing your percentage to an amount below 70%. A general rule would be to drop the percentage by 5% for every additional two months of hold time that you anticipate.

For example if you anticipate that your hold time will be 6–7 months you should reduce the formula percentage to 65% and it would look like this:

(After Repair Value X 65%) - Repair Cost = Maximum Price

On the other hand, if you can avoid the use of hard money you can increase the formula percentage. If you are able to use conventional financing, cash or if you have an investor funding the deal you may wish to increase the percentage to 75%. That formula would look like this:

(After Repair Value X 75%) - Repair Cost = Maximum Price

Of course, the objective is to pay as little as possible. These formulas are a guide to give you the maximum allowable price in order to have an excellent chance of turning a profit.

In summary, finding a good deal is hard work. If you find yourself walking away from the majority of deals you should understand that that is a good thing. It is human nature to want to jump in and get going; you need to resist that impulse. The most important thing to remember is that you make your money when you buy, not when you sell. The sale is when you realize your profit but you actually make it by buying at the right price. You may find yourself looking at so many bad deals that you almost will not believe it when you find one that actually works. That being said, when you do find that truly good deal, you need to jump on it before someone else does.

Summary

- Determine After Repair Value (ARV)

- Estimate Repairs Needed

- Estimate Time to Needed Complete Repairs

- Estimate Time Needed to Sell

- Estimate Financing Cost

- Use Formula: (ARV * 70%) - Repairs = Maximum Price

A Rehabber's Tale

Tony & Danny

After completing the sale of the property that we did as a joint venture, Tony started looking for his next deal. Tony had a friend Danny who was looking to get into real estate investing as well. They decided to apply some of the knowledge that they gained from a real estate training course they had taken by locating a deal through unconventional means. Instead of using a real estate agent to find a deal they decided to hunt for a motivated seller.

They drove through neighborhoods looking for neglected or abandoned homes. After scouring the area and creating a list they proceeded to contact the county recorder in order to locate the owner. They obtained the name and mailing address of each property owner as well as any other information that they could gather. With this information in hand they wrote letters to several homeowners to see if they would have an interest in selling their house.

They received several responses, some were curious while a few others were seriously interested in selling. One response was from a woman who lived in another state and had inherited the house when her mother died. A friend in the area had a key and Tony made arrangements to look at the house. The house was a little larger than most in the area and, while it needed a fair amount of work, was in decent shape. Tony asked me to look at the house with him and together we went over the scope of work needed and approximate cost.

Together with Danny, Tony went about crafting an offer to the seller. They knew that the owner was motivated to sell because she did not want to deal with the property and she was willing to accept any fair offer. The woman said that she thought she would be able to get about $90,000 but was aware that she would have to do a lot of work to get that price. Tony felt the house could command a price above $100,000 if it was fixed up properly. He expected to put about $15,000–$20,000 into the rehab. Tony and Danny did not have an abundance of cash on hand so they would attempt to get the seller to finance the property as well. They presented an offer of $55,000 with no money down and the seller to hold a note for two years. They also asked for the payments to be deferred for six months while they completed the rehab. Instead of receiving an expected counter offer they were surprised when the seller accepted their offer as-is. They were in business. Not only did they get their price, they avoided a down payment and the cost of financing while they completed the project.

As the excitement of getting the deal wore off, it was time to face reality, they had a lot of work to do and they both lived 250 miles away. Managing this project effectively was going to be the key to making a profit. They had an idea of what needed to be done but it took time to get the specifics nailed down and get started. The house was still furnished and had many items of value that were included in the sale. In an effort to dispose of these items, and to make some cash as well, they held a yard sale and called in a local antique dealer to see what they could sell. They did very well at the sale and earned some cash that they could put toward the rehab. They had a dumpster brought in and hired a crew to clean out the remaining items.

The house was in need of a new roof, paint inside and out, two new bathrooms and some work in the kitchen. They also decided to create a new closet and do some other basic renovations. There was also a small building in the back that needed to be knocked down and hauled away. They called in local contractors to get estimates and figured out what they could do themselves. The one thing that they hadn't counted on was that there were very few contractors in the area and, as a result, they were all busy and very expensive. Many of these contractors wouldn't be able to start working on the project for several months at best. They had to find another way.

Tony and Danny expanded the list of things that they would do themselves. While they had never done many of these things before, they would learn on the job. They found a neighbor with a backhoe who was willing to help them knock down the building in the rear. They brought in crews from the Las Vegas area to handle the painting and the roofing and they improvised where they could. While it was more expensive to do things this way, they saved a lot of time. Even with all of these efforts the project was well behind schedule. They were also way over budget and running out of money. Despite all of these problems they still managed to find a way to get the job done. They kept going when others might have given up and managed to finish the project just as they were due to start making payments.

They were significantly over their budget estimate, so in an effort to save some money they decided to attempt to sell the house themselves. If they couldn't find a buyer in a reasonable amount of time they would list the property with a real estate agent. They managed to find someone who was looking for a house in the area to use as a vacation home. When checking the comps on recent home sales they found that they would be able to get over $120,000 which was a lot more than they had expected. Their total cost including purchase, closing costs, rehab expenses, carrying costs and selling expenses, wound up being about $95,000. With a net sale price of $120,000 they had a profit of $25,000 to split. In addition to being a great lesson in rehab, it was also an excellent money maker.

Chapter 7

Making the Purchase

The greatest risk is not taking one.—**Anon**

If you've determined that you may have a good deal, you need to prepare your offer. You need to realize that a real estate transaction is not like making a purchase at a department store. There will be offers and counter-offers and negotiation. It is very much a give and take process to come up with a deal that both sides are comfortable with.

Offer Components

There are two primary components to any offer, price and terms. The assumption is that a seller will sell for the highest possible price. In many cases that is correct, but not always. Many distressed buyers are more concerned with the terms. They may need a quick close to avoid foreclosure or there may be other issues that the seller is concerned with. One of the major terms that could entice a seller is accepting the house in as-is condition. Many sellers of distressed properties are well aware that they will have to make concessions due to the condition of the property and may have difficulty selling at all. A buyer who will make an as-is offer may well have the upper hand in negotiations.

If you are making an as-is offer you need to be very careful in order to avoid costly mistakes, there may be things wrong that you aren't expecting.

If you are working with an agent you will have the agent submit the offer to the seller's agent. The offer will contain a period of time in which to respond or the offer will no longer be valid. Usually the seller will then submit a counter offer. This is why it is important to have items in the offer that are not very important to you so that you have something to give back in the negotiating phase. An offer is almost never considered to be "take it or leave it" except occasionally in a very hot or very cold market. By having items in the offer that are not important to you, you can concede these points. You need to create a win-win scenario where the buyer feels that he is being treated fairly.

Once you have decided on the terms, the next step is to determine what the house is worth to *you*. The mistake that a lot of people make, especially inexperienced investors, is to base their offer on what the owner is asking. Pay attention: W*hat the owner is asking is irrelevant!* The only price that matters is the one that you are willing to pay. Many people get hung up on the asking price; they think that because the owner is asking $250,000 they should offer $225,000. But what if the house is only worth $175,000? This is one mistake that I have seen people make over and over.

Determining Value

So how do you determine what the house is worth to you? You start by getting "comps" which are the sales prices for similar, or comparable, houses that have sold recently in the same vicinity. The more recent the data and the more like the house you are looking at, the more accurate the comp will be. If you are looking at a 1200 square foot 3 bedroom, 1 bath house, it would not be accurate if you compared it to a 5 bedroom, 3 bath house that was 2500 square feet. Getting comparable prices is not an exact science due to the variations from house to house. Even in a neighborhood where all houses were the same at first, they will now have very different prices based on the updates made to individual houses over the years. If you are working with a real estate agent, that person should be able to give you those sales figures. If you aren't, then you would need to look at the county records of recent sales to come up with the prices.

After you've determined what the house would be worth if it were in good condition (After Repair Value) then you need to determine how much work it needs to get it back into good condition. These repairs constitute the scope of work. You need to put a price on this that is as accurate as possible. Be sure to increase this number by 10–20% to allow for unexpected items.

When you have this number you can refer to the formula that we discussed earlier:

(After Repair Value x 70%) - Repairs = Maximum Offer

The maximum offer is just that, the most you will pay. You should certainly offer less at first so that you have some room to negotiate. You have a much better chance of making a deal if the owner feels like you gave in to him a little. Sometimes your lower first offer might even be accepted without a counter and that just gives you a greater profit potential.

So let's use an example. You've determined that the house you are looking at would sell for about $150,000 if it was in good condition. You estimate that the repairs will be $25,000 and you add in another $5,000 (20%) to cover unexpected items for a total of $30,000.

($150,000 x 70%) - $30,000 = Maximum Offer

$105,000 - 30,000 = $75,000 Maximum Offer

Your first offer should be for less than this amount. If you can't make a deal for $75,000 or less then you should walk away and look for another deal. Do not try to justify numbers that do not work in order to make something happen; that is a sure-fire way to lose money.

Making the Offer

So you've determined your maximum price, how do you actually make an offer? If you are working with an agent then the agent will handle that for you. Do not listen to an agent who tells you that the offer is too low or that the seller will not accept it. An agent is required to submit all offers regardless of what their opinion might be. It is up to the seller to accept or reject it.

If you are not working with an agent, then you need to find out if there is a standard offer form in your state. If so, you should use it so that you don't have problems later. If there is no agent involved, then you can submit your offer to the seller directly, otherwise the agent will present the offer. The seller should have a specified period of time to accept or reject the offer otherwise the offer will become void.

Many inexperienced homebuyers worry about insulting a seller with an offer that is too low. My answer to them is to ask why the seller wasn't embarrassed by asking too much. Remember you should offer what the property is worth to *you*.

Contingencies

You need to be sure that your offers protect your interests as well. Any offer to purchase should have contingencies in place that will allow you to back out without penalty if they are not met. What kinds of contingencies are important? Any offer should always be subject to the buyer being able to obtain financing at a specified rate for a specified period of time, for example: 30 year fixed rate a 6.5% interest. If you cannot obtain financing, you have the option to cancel the deal without penalty. An exception to this would be an *all cash* offer. An all cash offer can help you get a deal because the buyer does not have to depend on your ability to obtain financing and he may be willing to accept a lower price.

Another clause would be for inspections acceptable to the buyer. These inspections can be for structure, termites and other pests, mold, and any other concerns. Contractor repair estimates might be another item to consider. The important thing is to be careful and to leave yourself an escape clause if you need to back out of a deal. There will be a time frame in which the buyer is to complete all inspections and to perform any other due-diligence that may be necessary.

If this is an income property, you want to have a contingency clause allowing for the inspection of financial documents, leases and tax returns. You want to verify the accuracy of the numbers that the seller is giving you. Are the maintenance numbers in line with what you expect? Can the tenant leases be verified? Do the numbers for vacancy, utilities, insurance and other expenses check out? Income property will typically have expenses that amount to 40–50% of gross rents. If the amounts shown are significantly below that, you need to look at the numbers very carefully. Be sure to include expenses for professional management, even if you plan to manage the property yourself. Management fees typically run 8–10% of the rent collected. It is quite common for a seller of an income property to overstate income and understate expenses, the higher the profit that can be shown, the greater the price a seller can command. It is your job to be sure the numbers are correct; do not take them at face value.

Closing Date

Another item in the offer is the scheduled date to close escrow. The date that you set can have a great impact on the willingness of the seller to accept your offer. Frequently the buyer needs to sell as quickly as possible, so a rapid close can give you an edge in negotiations. Sometimes a seller may need to delay a close. Perhaps he needs time to locate another property or needs to delay the transfer for tax reasons. If you have been able to uncover the seller's motivation, you could be able to set a closing date that will greatly increase your odds of getting a deal.

Seller Concession

You may wish to ask for the seller to contribute towards the closing costs, this is also known as a *seller's concession*. Lenders will allow this contribution, but will generally place limits on the amount. Typically a seller can contribute up to 3% towards closing costs if you are making a 5% down payment, or up to 6% if you are making a down payment of 10% or more. The recent upheaval in the mortgage industry may change the requirements of many lenders and no assumptions should be made about this. You need to check with the lenders to see what they will allow.

You may be thinking that having the seller contribute to closing costs is the same as a price reduction. To the seller it is, but it can be more valuable to the buyer. By having the seller pay a portion of the closing costs the buyer will be able to put more cash in to the down payment, which effectively increases the down payment percentage. This can make a difference in getting the loan approved and can possibly eliminate PMI charges or reduce the PMI premium.

If the goal is to reduce or eliminate PMI, you can change the numbers after the deal is agreed upon. Let's say that you have reached an agreement on a price of $200,000. You can then request that the seller raise the price and credit the increase to the closing costs. You might change the price to $210,000 with the seller contributing $10,000 to your closing costs. The seller nets exactly the same amount but you are able to add $10,000 to the down payment. It will not change the amount of the mortgage but it will change the percentage of the down payment.

```
Original Deal

Price              =  $200,000

Down Payment       =    20,000

Mortgage           =   180,000

Percentage Down =       10%


Revised Deal

Price              =  $210,000

Down Payment       =    30,000

Mortgage           =   180,000

Percentage Down =     14.29%
```

As you can see, the mortgage amount is exactly the same. The seller will net the same amount from the sale. In effect you are only moving numbers around on paper but it could make a difference in meeting the loan qualification requirements, could change the PMI fees, or, in some cases, eliminate them entirely. You will usually do this if it is necessary for some reason since it does not change the net effect for the buyer or seller.

Counter Offers

After your offer has been submitted to the seller, he will have a period of time in which to respond. This is typically five business days but it can actually be any number that you set. What you do not want to do is to leave the offer open-ended. The deadline will put pressure on the seller to make a decision. Most offers will not be accepted as written. Sometimes they will be outright rejected as unacceptable, but more often the seller will present a *counter offer*. When you receive a counter offer the negotiations are usually just beginning.

It is possible that the counter offer is very close to what you originally offered. Perhaps some minor terms such as close of escrow date or some minor conditions or contingencies were the only changes. In this case it might be wise to simply accept the counter offer. If you do, you are on your way to a deal and can proceed to open escrow.

Negotiations

If you are still too far apart to accept the counter offer, you have to begin negotiating individual items. This is very much a give and take process. Every time that you concede some point or give something up you should ask for something in return. Even if you are only asking for something minor, you are conditioning the seller that he will have to give you something if he wants something from you. If you just give in to the seller's requests, he will frequently come up with additional requests. Requesting something in return will usually keep this from happening.

When it comes to money, a common practice in negotiations is to split the difference. A good negotiator can turn this in his favor while a poor negotiator can have it used against him. If you are negotiating with someone who likes to split the difference you can come out way ahead. If you do it right you can keep re-splitting the difference and have the number wind up much closer to your price. Frequently a seller will submit a counter offer that sets a price in the expectation that you will meet him halfway. If you do that he will get the price he is looking for. If you don't play along you can come out way ahead.

We'll assume that a seller is asking $230,000 for a property. You have done your homework and determine that the most you will pay is $210,000. You want to leave negotiating room so you make an offer of $190,000 which puts the price you are willing to pay right in the middle of the asking price and your offer. At this point the seller may come back with a counter offer that splits the difference or $210,000. Since this is what you were willing to pay, you could accept it, or you could try for a better deal.

Let's say that instead of accepting the price of $210,000, you counter back with an offer of $196,000. If the seller really needs to sell now and is not an experienced negotiator, he may come back with another counter offer that splits the difference yet again at a price of $203,000. You might then counter back again at $198,000; and you will probably wind up agreeing to a price of about $200,000. This is $10,000 less than you were originally willing to pay.

This scenario illustrates another point as well: When you are involved in back and forth negotiations over money, your moves should be smaller than the moves made by the seller. In our example the seller came down $20,000, but you only came up $6,000. In the second round the seller reduced his price by $7,000 but you only increased your offer by $2,000. Every round of offers moved the deal much closer to your price. Just because the seller moves in big jumps doesn't mean that you should.

Asking Price	= $230,000
1st Offer	= $190,000
Seller's Counter Offer	= 210,000
2nd Offer	= $196,000
Seller's Counter Offer	= 203,000
3rd Offer	= $198,000
Seller's Counter Offer	= 200,000
Agreed Upon Sales Price	= $200,000

Another point in negotiating price is to avoid the use of round numbers. Round numbers tend to have less impact. Going back to the example above, let's say that instead of an initial offer of $190,000 you made an offer of $190,250. This makes it appear that there is some rational basis to your offer instead of just picking a number because it sounds good. You may find that this will move a seller to your number very quickly. This is assuming that the seller is truly motivated to make a deal. He may move quickly for fear of losing you as a buyer.

Will every negotiation go this way? Of course not. The example above is being used to illustrate how negotiations *can* go. How things move along will depend on the motivation of the buyer and seller. Whoever is more motivated to make a deal will move the most. This is why you look for highly motivated and desperate sellers. They will give a tremendous amount of ground because they are afraid of losing the deal.

Emotions

Emotions play a huge part in any sales process. Think of times where your emotions have gotten the better of your logic. This is where buyer's remorse comes from. Have you ever made a deal only to regret it after the fact? Every car salesman in the world knows this. They want you to look at that shiny new automobile, get behind the wheel and smell the new leather. They want you to go for a test drive and get emotionally attached to the car so that you absolutely have to have it. If they can engage your emotions, you will exceed the price that you said you wouldn't go past. It is human nature and it happens to all of us.

Real estate is no different. Your ability to make a good deal will be in direct proportion to your ability to keep your emotions out of it. When you determine your maximum price for a property, you must be absolutely prepared to walk away. Many novice investors get so caught up in the desire to do a deal that they go past the maximum that they have set. It's easy to rationalize this by saying, "It's only a little more" or "I'll make it up somewhere else." This is a recipe for disaster. If you can't make a deal at your price you should walk away and start looking for the next deal.

There are many books available on the art of negotiating. It would be a good idea to read a few and put what you learn into practice. Improved negotiating skills will lead to better deals. Remember, you make your money when you buy. If you buy it right you will come out ahead the vast majority of the time.

Acceptance

If the price and terms have been agreed upon, you may be thinking that you have a deal. What you have is not a deal but *acceptance*, your offer has been accepted by the seller. At this point the deal is still not complete. It is time to open escrow and begin the process of attempting to meet the contingencies. If the contingencies are met, and everything moves to a close, then you have a deal.

Now it is time to put in the application for financing and order whatever inspections have been agreed to. Your lender will begin the investigation of title and order the necessary appraisals. If the title report and appraisal meet the standards of the lender, the loan will be approved and they will prepare to fund the purchase.

Home Inspection

One of your contingencies should be that the purchase is contingent upon a home inspection report acceptable to the buyer. A contingency worded this way will allow you to back out of just about any deal if you need to. I recommend getting an inspection done in just about every case. While you can't count on a home inspector to find everything, it is quite possible that he will find things that you would not. If the inspector finds something that you didn't, he may have saved you a lot of money and headaches. Even if you have a lot of construction experience, the inspector may still have a different way of looking at things.

What a Home Inspector Looks For

Exterior:

Roof

Chimney

Gutters

Foundation

Bricks/Mortar

Windows

Landscape & Drainage

Interior:

Plumbing

Drains, faucets & water pressure

Electric

Heat

Air Conditioning

Fireplace

Leaks

Doors

Stairs

Ceiling Fans

The inspector should have a report to you in a matter of days.

Re-negotiation

The inspection report is your opportunity to negotiate additional concessions from the seller. If the seller is really motivated to complete the deal, he will not want to let the inspection report stop it from happening. If the inspection uncovered any major problems that you were unaware of, you may want to walk away altogether. It is more likely that the report will uncover some things that will get the seller to agree to drop the price a little more. If the seller has reached his lowest price limit, and refuses to come down any further you will have to decide whether it is worth it for you to proceed.

When everything has been agreed to, and all of the inspections have been completed, and any contingencies have been met, then, and only then, you have a deal. You are now ready to proceed to the next step and close escrow.

Closing Escrow

If everything has been taken care of properly then closing escrow should be a fairly simple step. When all of the contingencies have been met and last minute details have been worked out, then the escrow officer will have the closing documents prepared. The settlement document, called the HUD1, will be prepared showing the financial aspects of the transaction for each side.

By this time the Title Company will have completed the title search to be sure that the title is free of liens or judgments, known as clouds on title, and that the deed can be transferred. Sometimes there are issues that need to be clarified prior to the deed being transferred. There may be one or more liens on a property that should have been released earlier but haven't been. Most of these issues are minor and are cleared up well in advance of closing.

There is always the possibility that someone else has a valid claim to the property due to an error at some point in time. To protect the buyer against such an occurrence the Title Company will issue a *title insurance policy*. In the event that there was an undiscovered claim and someone else is the rightful owner of the property, the title insurance will pay the claim so that the buyer isn't harmed financially. This is an incredibly rare event, and as such title insurance is relatively inexpensive, but you wouldn't want to be without it. The buyer or the seller can pay the title insurance policy premium. Local custom usually dictates who pays, but it is a negotiable item.

On some occasions, a dispute may arise during the close of escrow. This usually happens because there was a misunderstanding on some point or because someone didn't take care of something properly. If there are attorneys involved in the transaction then they will usually work things out. If there are no attorneys, then it is up to all of the parties involved to resolve the issue.

Once everything is complete and the money changes hands, the deal is done. If there is a loan involved then you may have to wait for the lender to fund the deal for it to be complete. When the money has transferred and the papers are signed you will get your keys. Congratulations, you now own the house.

Are you ready to get to work?

Summary

- Determining Value

- Offers

- Contingencies

- Seller Concessions

- Counter Offers

- Negotiations

- Home Inspections

A Rehabber's Tale

Minna

Minna Javanainen (minnaj@comcast.net) had been working in a sales position as an account manager in Connecticut. While the position paid well, it involved travel and time away from her family and it was ultimately unsatisfying. To make matters worse, the company she worked for had been bought out and her job responsibilities would be changing. She had always wanted to invest in real estate and she loved remodeling so she thought that rehabbing homes would be ideal for her. She had set a goal of investing in real estate by the time she was 30 years old; she was now 29 so why not get started?

She formed her company, New England Home Solutions, LLC, and began advertising to find distressed sellers. She placed ads in newspapers and used bandit signs saying "We Buy Houses" and eventually she received a call from a couple in Colchester, CT, who were looking to sell their single family home. Minna looked at the house and estimated that it would take about two weeks to renovate at a cost of about $12,000. She negotiated a purchase price of $162,000 and closed the deal in February 2007. She had her first rehab!

Minna soon found out that rehabbing is not as easy as it seems on TV.

> **Minna:** "I was terrified of the whole thing. I was sure I had gone out on a ledge and destined myself to go bust. Closing cost much more than I anticipated. Then what had seemed like a light cosmetic rehab turned into something much more. The further I got, the more problems surfaced. One day we found an odd lump in the ceiling and opened it up. We found a cracked joist. When we started looking around, they kept surfacing. I was sure the house had a major structural problem. The ceiling was half torn out. Then the furnace stopped working. It was February in New

England. I very distinctively remember that next very horrid day when I came to the house in the morning. It was freezing cold. I looked around at my disaster of a torn apart house and wondered what I had done to myself. It got worse when I headed into the basement and found that the plumber had gotten a little lazy and the basement was flooded. I was completely over-whelmed. I had counted on a two week project and I was at two weeks and I wasn't even done painting yet, never mind anything else. I thought I was doomed.

But it got better. The next few days and weeks were long. I encountered more problems ... problems with my people not showing up, problems with the inspector approving what I had done, a climate that wouldn't cooperate, faulty wiring, unleveled rooms, crazy carpenter bees, a well no-one could find, water that smelled like rotten eggs.... but I just kept work-ing. Seven weeks later, the house was done. It was beautiful. To tell you the truth, I wanted to live there. But I needed my money out. The house went on the market. There were some showings. Every nasty com-ment was a personal insult to my 'masterpiece.' After three weeks on the market I thought no one would make an offer and I'd be moving in, but like magic I got a full price offer with no contingencies."

Like many new rehabbers, Minna ran into problems she hadn't expected. A project that she thought she could complete in two weeks wound up taking seven, and her $12,000 budget had ballooned to $33,000. She managed the project and was there every day for the seven-week duration of the job, doing a lot of the work herself. She was in a real estate market that was beginning to soften and was anx-ious about getting the house sold before the carrying costs ate away her profit. She priced the house aggressively at $264,000 and it sat on the market for three tense weeks before she found a buyer. The sale closed a few weeks later and she had a net profit of $40,000.

In addition to a nice profit, Minna gained valuable experience from her first rehab.

> **Minna:** "I really didn't have too much of an idea of what I had gotten into. Looking back, the biggest challenge I faced was finishing the project in a time and cost effective manner and getting it sold quickly. I kind of slapped it all together as we went along. Now I'd have a solid plan. But knowing how to do that comes with experience, which I didn't have at the time.
>
> A lot of people want to 'flip' houses. In fact almost every single one that I've ever told the story of that rehab house says, 'I've always wanted to do that!' A lot of people dream. Few people do. I think those who dream and then do are the ones who are most successful in this world, in or outside real estate. Rehabbing is certainly not for everyone, and it's not easy, but I think a lot of people who could be successful just sit on that fence forever and never jump off. I'm not big on regret … sometimes you just have to take that risk and go for what you want. You may do something great. You may fail miserably. But you'll never know if you don't try. But always—BUY RIGHT. If you buy right, you'll have a very hard time failing."

Minna is well on her way and has many more rehabs in her future.

Chapter 8

Financing the Deal

Money is better than poverty, if only for financial reasons.—**Woody Allen**

So you've found a property to rehab; now you have to pay for it. There are many different ways to fund a typical real estate purchase, but rehab is a different animal. If the rehab is minor, perhaps only cosmetic or small repairs, you might be able to use conventional financing sources through banks and mortgage lenders. But, if it is like many rehab properties, the traditional lenders will not touch it. These sources only want to provide mortgage loans for everyday properties to your typical homebuyer. They do not understand the rehab marketplace, nor do they want to.

If traditional sources will not touch it, what do you do? There are many different options to choose from depending on the circumstances. Some of these options require that you have good credit while others do not. Some sources require that you invest a substantial amount of your own capital but others don't. Many sources of capital have a difficult approval process yet others are relatively simple. Which one is best? The answer is that it depends, the borrower's circumstances matter in some cases while not in others. Where you go really depends on the situation that you are facing. Let's explore some of these options.

Cash Purchase

The simplest way to buy a property is to just pay cash. That might work on a property that is cheap enough or if the buyer happens to have a lot of idle cash on hand. Of course, that usually isn't the case. Buying a property with cash makes for a very easy transaction with little or no red tape to deal with. Being a cash buyer can also give you an edge over any other competing buyers. A seller is more likely to accept a cash offer over an offer involving financing because they know that the deal is more likely to close. This is especially true in the case of a seller who is trying to sell a distressed property. Distressed properties pose a challenge for sellers because buyers are unable to get approved for traditional mortgages and are unaware of other financing methods or unwilling to take that route. There is definitely truth to the saying that "cash is king."

HELOC

What if you could be a cash buyer without having any cash? If you have equity in your home or other investment properties it may be possible to use it. You could refinance your current mortgage or add a second mortgage. A very good way may be to use a home equity line of credit or HELOC. A HELOC has several advantages over refinancing or taking out a second mortgage. A HELOC frequently costs very little, if anything, in the form of closing costs. If you take the HELOC on an investment property, you may have to pay for an appraisal or other costs but it is still less expensive than a refinance or second mortgage in most cases. The rate on a HELOC will typically be higher and is based on an index, such as the prime rate, so the rate will vary as the index changes. Another advantage is in the very nature of a line of credit; you only use what you need, when you need it. You can take the money out as the money as needed, and pay it back when the rehab project is sold. When you are ready for your next project, it is there to be used again.

There are disadvantages to a HELOC as well. The rate will vary based on the fluctuation of the index. This means that your payments can change and it could wind up costing you more than expected each month. The money is readily available in the form of checks and, in some cases, credit cards. This may tempt some people into using the money for things other than what was originally intended. Still, if it is used responsibly, this can be a great way to finance your rehab ventures.

Seller Financing

Another way to avoid dealing with the usual lending sources is to have the seller carry back financing. This can be done pretty easily if the seller owns the property outright, that is, the seller has no mortgage loan on the property. While this is not the norm, it does happen often enough. In a case like this it is possible to make a deal with the seller in which you give a small down payment or maybe even no down payment at all. The seller will receive payments from you at a stated rate of interest for a specified period of time. The terms may include a balloon payment that is due at a certain date. An example would be that you buy a house for $100,000 with a 10% down payment ($10,000) at an interest rate of 8% for 30 years with a 5-year balloon. In plain English this means that you give the seller $10,000 when you buy the house and then make payments to him based on a $90,000 mortgage with a payment term of 30 years and an interest rate of 8%. The 5-year balloon means that the remaining balance of the loan is to be paid at the end of 5 years. You can pay the mortgage off by selling the house or refinancing the loan prior to the due date of the balloon payment.

There are a number of reasons why a seller would be willing to carry back financing on the house. If the house is in poor condition, it will be easier for the seller to find a buyer if he offers a financing option. The seller could be in a position where the thought of receiving a monthly check is appealing. It could also be a benefit for him in terms of taxes if the transaction is treated as an installment sale. When looking at properties it is always a good idea to ask if seller financing is available.

It is also possible for a seller to carry back some financing even if he does have a mortgage on the house. If the seller has a large amount of equity in the property he may be willing to take some or all of it in the form of a mortgage. Let's use the same example of a $100,000 purchase price but this time we'll assume that the seller owes $50,000 on a mortgage. The buyer could obtain a first mortgage loan for $50,000 and the seller could carry back a 2nd mortgage for all or part the balance. The buyer would make two payments each month, one to the primary lender and another to the seller. A seller 2nd is actually quite common in cases where there is a lot of equity involved. The primary lender may have rules concerning how much a seller may carry back. Lenders tend to be concerned if a buyer has little or no money of his own tied up in a deal.

The idea here is to be a little creative and think outside of the box. I know of one situation where an investor was buying a rehab property that the seller had inherited and just wanted to get rid of. He made an offer based on what he was willing to pay. He also asked the seller to hold a note with no money down and no payments for 6 months with a balloon payment due in two years. The seller accepted without even a counter offer. The buyer had six months to rehab and sell the property. He wound up making a very nice profit with no money out of his pocket other than rehab costs. He never expected the seller to accept this offer but he made it anyway. This time it worked perfectly, other times it could be a place to start a negotiation. The point is that you don't know if you don't ask.

Subject To Existing Loan

Another way to buy a property without having to obtain a mortgage is to purchase it "subject to existing financing." This can be a risky way to do it because you are essentially leaving the mortgage in the seller's name. The bank is not notified about the sale so that the "due on sale" clause is not triggered. Unless a loan is designated as an assumable loan, it is supposed to be paid off when the title is transferred. The seller is taking a risk because the loan remains in their name; if the buyer doesn't pay and a foreclosure takes place it appears, on the seller's credit report. Why would a seller agree to this? The usual answer is that the seller is desperate. If foreclosure is looming and there is no buyer in sight then a "subject to" deal may be a viable option.

From a buyer's perspective, in order for this kind of deal to make sense there must be enough equity in the property to make it profitable.

The seller will usually expect to get some cash but not always. After the title is transferred the buyer becomes the legal owner of the property and can do whatever they wish with it. The usual idea is to rehab it and sell it for profit. When the sale is made the mortgage that is still in the seller's name is paid off.

Let's use an example. We'll assume that a property has an After Repair Value (ARV) of $300,000 and needs $30,000 in repairs. Using our formula we determine that we are willing to pay $180,000.

(ARV x 70%) - Repairs = Maximum Offer

($300,000 x 70%) - $30,000 = Maximum Offer

$210,000 - 30,000 = $180,000 Maximum Offer

For our example we'll assume that the foreclosure sale is about to happen and the seller would need to bring the loan current and pay the legal costs associated with the foreclosure action in order to halt the process and reinstate the loan. If the loan balance was $150,000 and the amount needed to reinstate the loan was $10,000 in payment arrears and costs, the seller would have a total indebtedness of $160,000.

If we were to agree on a price of $180,000, we would need $30,000 in cash since we are keeping the existing mortgage. We would use $10,000 to bring the loan current, leaving $20,000 to be paid to the seller. The reason a seller would agree to this is that they are about to lose their home and would most likely be left with nothing. In a case like that, $20,000 could be enough to help then get a fresh start. In this type of scenario it is a good idea for the seller to walk away with some money. If they are faced with the prospect of selling their house and walking away with nothing, they may feel that this is just as bad as a foreclosure.

From a buyer's perspective the primary risk is that the lender learns about the transfer and invokes the "due on sale" clause. The mortgage documents clearly state that the loan is to be repaid upon sale except in case where it is an assumable loan. If the loan is not paid, then the lender will start the foreclosure process. The amount of time it actually takes to foreclose on a house varies from state to state but it is usually at least four months and in many cases longer. The length of the fore-closure process gives you time to complete the rehab and sell or refi-nance the property. The reality is that most lenders will not know that the property has changed hands if the payments are current. If a loan goes into default status they will check the ownership at that time.

How you actually hold title in a subject-to deal varies from state to state. In some cases it should be held in a land trust, in others an LLC. If you plan on using this method, you should learn as much as possible about the local laws. While it may not be illegal to do these deals, you are circumventing the rules of the mortgage and need to consider the various risks involved as well as ethical considerations.

Conventional Loan

If you do not have the resources to pay cash or are unable to get the seller to finance the deal, you need to obtain a loan to complete the pur-chase. If possible, you should try to finance the purchase using a con-ventional mortgage. There are many types available including fixed and adjustable rates for a variety of different repayment periods, the most common being a 30-year term. The down payments can vary by lender from nothing down to the traditional 20%. If you use little or no down payment, you may be required to carry Private Mortgage Insurance or PMI. PMI will protect the lender in a case where the buyer defaults and the lender cannot recover the full loan amount through the foreclosure process. The PMI premium is paid by the borrower and is added to the monthly mortgage payment. When the borrower has a certain amount of equity built up, he can request that the PMI be dropped.

As mentioned earlier, getting a conventional loan for a rehab proj-ect can be difficult. The lender will order an appraisal, which will list defects that are found in addition to placing a value on the house. Some are deal killers while others aren't. If the problems are not too bad, the lender may require that money be set aside in escrow to cover the costs of any repairs that may be necessary. If the repairs are mostly cosmetic in nature, you could be ok. Things like paint, carpet, cleaning up the landscaping and other minor items should not stop you from getting a loan. Other things such as major plumbing and electrical problems, foundation issues, a bad roof or other major items could be enough to make a lender decline a loan.

Just as there are closing costs when you purchase the house, there are also costs involved in obtaining a loan. Some of these costs are paid up front in the form of an application fee and appraisal fee. These fees are generally not refundable if you are not approved. Therefore it is better to have an idea as to whether or not the property itself qualifies before you even apply. A good loan officer should be able to give you the lender's criteria prior to submitting an application. You need to be aware that there is a tendency among mortgage professionals to claim that they can do anything. Remember that they usually do not get paid unless they actually close a loan and they do not want you going to a competitor. So be wary of someone who makes promises that sound too good to be true.

Hard Money

Since we are talking about rehab it is highly likely that the property will not qualify for a conventional loan. If that is the case, what do you do? One option is to use lenders that specialize in difficult to place, or non-traditional loans. These are known as Hard Money Lenders (HML). Because these loans pose a significantly higher risk for the lender, you can expect to pay more in the form of higher rates, points and fees. Hard money loans are generally associated with borrowers who have bad credit but they really apply to any difficult to place loans.

How are rehab loans different? A traditional loan is based on the value of the property as well as the borrower's ability to repay. A rehab loan is based primarily on the value of the house after repairs are made. This is known as the *After Repair Value* or ARV. Most hard money lenders will offer loan amounts up to 65 or 70% of ARV. The cost of the repairs can be included in this amount. Let's say that you purchase a house with an ARV of $100,000, if the lender will allow 70% of ARV that means you can get a loan of $70,000. If the purchase price of the home is $50,000, you would be left with $20,000 for repairs ($70,000 - 50,000 = 20,000). Money that you borrow for repairs is usually held in an escrow account and disbursed to you in a series of draws as repairs are made.

The interesting point here is that by following our winning formula, (ARV x 70%) - Cost of Repairs = Maximum Price, you will rarely need to be putting in a lot of your own money. Using this formula will limit your purchase price to the maximum that you can borrow, repairs included. It should be noted, however, that many lenders would expect you to have some of your own money at risk until you have established a track record with them. This means that you may not be able to do a true no money down deal at first.

So now you know how much you can borrow; what is it going to cost? Since a rehab loan is a hard money loan, it is considered a high risk to the lender. This means that you can expect it to be expensive. First there will be points associated with the loan. A point is equal to 1% of the amount borrowed. On rehab loans to an experienced rehabber who has a track record with the lender, you can expect to pay about 4 points, or 4% of the amount borrowed. Someone who is new to rehabbing, or is dealing with the lender for the first time, can expect to pay 7 or more points. Each loan thereafter should have fewer points attached until the rehabber proves himself and qualifies for the lender's best rate.

In addition to points, you can expect to pay more in interest as well. At a time when the Prime rate is below 8% and conventional mortgages are in the 6–7% range, rehab loans will be in the range of 14–18%. While the rate is high, the loans are usually held for a very short period of time. The interest and points can often be rolled into the loan.

Because a hard money rehab loan is designed to be short-term money, the loan term is generally limited to 6–12 months. The idea is to borrow the money, rehab the property and sell. If you are going to hold any longer than that, you will need to refinance into a traditional loan. There are some rehab lenders that will go longer than 12 months, but most will not. There may also be additional fees involved to extend the loan.

Since rehab loans are based on the value of the house, the borrower's credit is not as big a factor as in other loans. That is not to say that credit is ignored altogether. The lender will usually run a credit report to look for red flags. They may not be willing to lend to someone who has had a significant number of credit problems but they will be much more lenient that traditional lenders.

While rehab loans make it possible to do deals that could not ordinarily be done, they add a large financial burden to the deal. If a project last 6 months from start to final sale the financing burden could easily be 10–15% of the total cost of the project.

Money Partner

Another option that has lower risk is to bring in an investment partner. I would much rather give up some of my profit than put myself at risk with hard money financing. There are plenty of people who see the profit potential of rehabs but do not have the necessary skills to do it themselves. By investing in a project they can earn a better return on their money than many other investments. How much they earn depends on the degree of involvement. If they lend all of the money, they can expect a better return than they can by lending a lesser amount. If they are guaranteed a minimum rate of interest, they can expect a smaller share of the final profit. If they do not receive a guarantee then they can expect a greater percentage of the profit.

What would be a fair split of the profits? Let's say that you do all of the work to find and acquire the property, and you manage the rehab and sale from start to finish; then a split of 60/40 might be acceptable. The 60% goes to you and 40% to the investors. While you did all the work, they assumed all of the risk. If the investors wanted a minimum guarantee, then they would be entitled to a smaller percentage at the end.

Using the 60/40 split and the $100,000 house in our example we can see how it works. The cost to purchase and repair the property is $70,000 which is loaned by the investor. The house is sold for $100,000 net, which results in a profit of $30,000. You receive 60% or $18,000 without having any money at risk. The investor earns 40% or $12,000 on his $70,000 investment but does none of the work. His return is 17%; if the project lasts for 6 months that is equivalent to a 34% annualized return. While the net result to you is similar to using a rehab loan, you have eliminated a major risk. If the project took longer than expected to complete or sell, your financing costs with a rehab loan would have increased greatly resulting in a significantly lower profit.

The split that was used here is only an example. The actual split is a negotiable item and should be fair to both parties. Having investment partners can make it much easier to complete deals. Having a ready source of capital can allow you to jump on deals that you might otherwise have to pass up. While you might be giving up some short-term profits, it could be a much more profitable scenario in the long run.

FHA 203k

There are other ways to finance projects as well, the Housing and Urban Development (HUD) agency has a rehab financing program called section 203(k). This program is currently available for owner occupants only and is designed for the purchase and rehab of 1–4 family properties. The rules on this program change from time to time. The best way to obtain more information is from the Web site www.hud.gov. There are other programs available for low-income housing and senior housing as well from various government agencies.

As you can see, there are many different ways to finance a deal. If a deal truly makes sense, you can find a way to make it happen. Many people assume that they cannot find financing when what they really should be asking themselves is *how* they can obtain financing. Many potential investors never ask the seller to finance, they just assume he won't. People come across good deals and let them pass by because they do not understand how to get it done. If you truly believe that a deal is good then find a way to make it happen.

Choosing a Lender

So how do you choose a lender? The marketplace is definitely confusing. You'll hear terms like *mortgage banker, mortgage broker, direct lender, hard money lender* and other variations of these. The biggest difference is whether a loan company is lending their own money or simply arranging financing through another party. You will hear arguments going both ways as to which is better, there are advantages and disadvantages to each.

Mortgage Banker

A *mortgage banker* or a *direct lender* is generally a mortgage company or bank that is lending its own money. The advantages to this method are that you are dealing directly with the lender and can often eliminate some red tape. Also you will sometimes get better terms, fees and rates than with other methods. The key word is "sometimes." Do not assume that because you are dealing with a bank or mortgage company directly that you will always get a better deal. Many banks and major lenders have wholesale and retail divisions. If you deal with them directly, you are working with the retail department. Their wholesale division will sell loan packages through other mortgage companies and brokers. These other firms get better rates than you will by dealing direct. The disadvantage of using mortgage bankers or direct lenders is that you are limited to the programs that they offer even though it may not be the best solution for you.

Mortgage Broker

A *mortgage broker* is someone who will work with many different lenders in an effort to find the best deal for your situation. A good mortgage broker will shop several sources to find the best deal for you; a bad mortgage broker will shop several sources to find the best deal for him. You need to do your homework and shop carefully. It's not all about the interest rate, although that is an important factor. The main advantage of using a mortgage broker is that he can shop multiple sources to find the deal that is best for you. The primary disadvantage is that you have to pay a broker fee. However, many brokers are able to get better rates on loans than you can get yourself and this savings can be equal to or greater than the fees charged.

Loan Fees

There are many ways that brokers and bankers can make money on loans. Some ways are pretty obvious, such as the charging of points and origination fees. Money can also be made through the adding on of "garbage" fees. When you look at the final loan documents at closing, you will see a lot of items such as courier fees, document fees, processing fees, credit report fee, underwriting fee and many other small charges that add up to more profit for the lender. Some fees are legitimate but others are just tacked on. It is possible to have the "junk" fees removed altogether and many of the legitimate fees reduced, so do not hesitate to question them.

Those are all fees and charges that are visible, what about the ones you can't see? Mortgage lenders can make money by marking up the interest rate on a loan. Many people are aware that automobile dealers can do this, but do not realize that it happens in the mortgage industry as well. If you have great credit and shop around and do your homework you have a good chance of getting a decent loan. On the other hand, if your credit has a few blemishes or your job history and other factors are spotty you may have a more difficult time getting a good mortgage.

There are a couple of terms that many mortgage lenders would prefer that you didn't know. They are "par rate" and "yield spread premium." The term *par rate* refers to the wholesale rate of the loan. This is the rate that the lender charges for the money. If the broker or loan officer charges you more than par rate, then the lender will pay them additional money when the loan closes. Lenders use charts or grids that will show them how much they pay for each increase in the interest rate. The difference between the par rate and the rate that you are charged is called the yield spread. The amount that the lender pays the brokers and loan officers for increasing the rate is called the *yield spread premium*. The problem is not that the lender is paying this money but that it is not disclosed. On some loans this yield-spread premium can be more than the fees that are disclosed. When you are dealing with ethical professionals, this is not a problem but when you are dealing with someone who does not have your best interest at heart you can be stuck with a very bad loan. If you wind up paying an extra ½% interest on a $100,000 loan, it could result in additional interest of more than $12,000 over the life of a 30-year mortgage. You may have a loan that looks like it is low in costs because the closing statement doesn't show a lot of fees, but there could be a yield spread premium that you don't see.

So the fees that are disclosed are not the problem, it is the undisclosed money that you pay that can cost you thousands. So how do you compare loans? When a mortgage company or bank quotes you an interest rate you will see two figures, an interest rate and the APR or annual percentage rate. The APR includes the interest rate plus the effect of points, origination fees and other charges over the life of the loan. It is possible for one loan to have a lower interest rate than another yet have a higher APR. When comparing loans you should be using the APR so that you get a true comparison based on all fees included.

You might then be tempted to conclude that the loan with the lowest APR is always the best, but that also is not always the case. The APR assumes that you will have the loan for the full term. In most cases, especially rehab, you will pay the loan off well before maturity because you sold the property or refinanced the loan. You need to look at your total out-of-pocket costs over the life of the loan. For this reason a mortgage with a much higher interest rate but much lower fees could actually be less expensive.

There is a new breed of mortgage professional emerging called *flat-fee brokers*. As the term implies, a flat-fee broker will help you obtain a loan and charge a set fee for doing so. The way a typical broker works, he will make more on a larger loan because he usually earns a percentage of the loan amount. There is not a lot of difference in the work required to obtain a $100,000 mortgage or a $500,000 mortgage yet the broker makes significantly more on the larger loan. A flat-fee broker will generally give you the loan at the par-rate and charge a fee for his services. You also have the ability to customize the loan by taking a higher interest rate and having the yield spread premium that is paid to the broker used to off-set his fee and other costs associated with the loan.

Summary

Financing Options:

- Cash

- HELOC

- Seller Financing

- Assuming Existing Loan

- Conventional Loan

- Hard Money

- Money Partner

- Government Programs

Working With Lenders:

- Mortgage Banker

- Mortgage Broker

- Flat-Fee Broker

A Rehabber's Tale

Cindy

Cindy works full-time as a fixed-income financial analyst for an institutional money manager. She had been living in New York City rental apartments for twenty years when she decided that it was time to get her own place. Having a house to call her own would also give her an outlet for her creative side. While she had a knack for decorating and remodeling, she felt limited by the walls of the apartments that didn't belong to her. So she began her search.

Cindy worked with a real estate agent and found a house to her liking in Greenwich, Connecticut. It was 2005 and the market was heavily in the favor of sellers and prices were rising sharply. The house was in need of an overhaul to bring it up to today's standards but she felt she was up to the challenge. Her offer of $635,000 was accepted and she closed the deal in June. Now it was time to get to work!

While Cindy used contractors for an electrical upgrade and major plumbing work, she handled much of the project herself. The renovations included a complete kitchen remodel with new stainless steel appliances, soapstone countertops and a copper farm sink, two new bathrooms, all new windows and doors and refinishing the wood floors. One of the high-impact changes was the removal of walls on the stairway to create a sense of openness with new balusters and Newell posts. New door, window, baseboard and crown molding was also installed. New lighting, outlets and wall switches were added and metal radiators were replaced with custom wood versions that also functioned as window seats. New paint throughout finished the interior work.

The exterior received its' share of attention as well. The existing landscaping was replaced with all new plants and shrubs. Brick pavers were used to create a backyard patio, which was topped off with a Pergola. The front and rear steps were refaced with slate and a tool shed was added for garden supplies. A cedar fence surrounding the property completed this part of the project. The end result of all of this was a house with stunning curb appeal.

> **Cindy:** "I looked upon the entire redo as more of a 'fun project' than something to be dreaded. Prior to this house, I had lived in NYC apartments for twenty years. Most of my apartments were rentals and there is only so much you can do within the four walls of an apartment to 'remodel.' Here I could actually make changes!!
>
> I am also an information junkie, so I researched EVERY single project I embarked on. I asked tons of 'how to' questions of experts on various internet forums, bought tons of books for ideas, and subscribed to every home magazine available. I was also a stickler for making sure I was getting the best price on supplies and labor.—I knew I had champagne taste on a beer budget, so I had to be especially strict with my budgets (dozens of spreadsheets, price comparison matrixes, etc.)"

Cindy encountered surprisingly few problems during the project. She says her biggest challenge was "Living in the mess (I lived here during the entire renovation)." Cindy purchased this house to be her home, not a flip, but she has listed it for $900,000. She spent a total of $80,000 on the renovations and will have a sizeable profit when she sells.

Cindy's foray into rehabbing was, according to her, a "complete fluke."

> **Cindy:** "As I was rehabbing my house for myself, I realized—'hey, I'm really good at this.' Rehabbing takes advantage of my inherent personality traits: sense of design, ability to work within tight budget, attention to detail, very resourceful, etc."

When she was asked what she would do differently, she responded "Since I didn't plan on this being a flip, I did not buy the house with 'rehab/profit' in mind. For my next purchase, profit analysis will be #1 criterion."

It appears that Cindy has found something that she is totally suited to.

> **Cindy:** "I will absolutely continue this 'hobby' in the future. In fact, I believe I've finally found my true passion. I also have found the perfect outlet to unleash my creativity while nurturing my tendency towards perfectionism. Finally, I'm a junkie for finding the bargains, so my love of shopping lets me add lots of high end finishes to the house without stretching my budget."

It looks like there will be many successful rehabs in Cindy's future!

Chapter 9

Managing the Project

*In preparing for battle I have always found that plans
are useless, but planning is indispensable.*
—**Dwight D. Eisenhower**

So you've purchased your rehab property, now what? If you did a
proper evaluation prior to making the purchase, you have a good idea
of what needs to be done. The first step is to figure out the scope of
work required. Is it a minor cosmetic rehab or a major gut and rebuild
project? Is it a-do-it-yourself project, or will you be bringing in contractors? Will you be doing some of the work and contracting the rest?
These are things that need to be carefully considered. You may be capa-
ble of doing all of the work but how long will it take you? You need to
remember that the clock is ticking, you may think that you can save
money by doing the bulk of the work yourself but you could find that
it costs you more because it takes you a lot longer to complete. If the
house needs to be fully or partially gutted you may think it's best to
do that part yourself. But if you hired people to help with that, you
might save more in time than it costs to pay the help. Ultimately this

is a decision that you need to make yourself. If you make the wrong decision, hopefully learn for next time.

Timeline

After figuring the scope of the project, you need to create a timeline. If you are working with a contractor, he will be able to help you to do this. Creating a proper timeline is an extremely important part of any rehab project. You need to coordinate different aspects of the job so that everything flows smoothly. Without a good idea of what needs to be done, and when, you will find yourself stopping and starting repeatedly. Remember that the clock is ticking and every delay costs you money. This is very important when ordering material and coordinating various contractors. You don't want to wait until the kitchen is ready for cabinets to order them, if you do, you might find yourself waiting for several weeks with nothing to do.

You also need to be able to multi-task; it is not unusual to have several things going on at once. You might have electricians and plumbers working inside and have roofers and a landscape crew working outside, all at the same time. You will find yourself wearing many hats and putting out many fires. You need to understand that this is all part of the job. Things can get very hectic when you have a project running and you need to keep on top of it all.

Contractors

If you are going to hire a contractor, how do you find a good one? The best way is to get recommendations from other people. Before hiring one of these referrals, you should see their work and talk to them to be sure that you are comfortable with them. Communication is very important; you need to be sure that they understand your needs and concerns. They need to be aware of your deadlines as well as your budget. Beware of contractors who low-ball the initial price only to find other things that need to be done as they go along. However, still understand that problems will pop up unexpectedly and additional work may be needed to correct them. Prior to hiring anyone, you should check with the state and local contractors' board to see if there are any complaints against the contractor and to verify that they have the proper licenses and insurance.

When working with contractors, you need to be aware that there can be difficulties. There are contractors who do not show up when they are supposed to or sometimes do not show up at all. They may be there for several days and then they are missing in action. It could be that they are working on several jobs simultaneously or need to go take care of a problem elsewhere. They may have priorities other than you. That is not to suggest that all contractors are like that, but some are. You need to be sure to communicate clearly and have things in writing as much as possible. You should never pay for a job that isn't completed. It is normal to provide a deposit when work starts, and have a payment schedule as work progresses, but something should always be held back until the job is completed to your satisfaction.

Sometimes things may not be done exactly as you think they should. Having a dispute with a contractor can hamper a project, so you need to pick your battles carefully. You may find it necessary to be diplomatic at times but you need to be willing to stand your ground if you feel an issue is important. The last thing you want to happen is for a contractor to walk off the job because the two of you do not see eye to eye. It all comes back to choosing your contractors carefully and communicating clearly.

Designing a Project

If you are doing a major renovation with structural changes, you may want to consult an architect. A professional in this area can offer advice as to what works best and draw up plans that will help you to acquire the necessary permits. Most rehab projects do not go this far, they just involve modernizing and repairing the existing structure. But do not hesitate to hire an architect if you need one, it could be well worth the added expense.

When doing an extensive renovation without the services of a professional architect, you may wish to use a home design software program. When using these programs, you input the dimensions and features of the property and use the software to plan changes. The software ranges from low end, low cost versions to extremely expensive professional architectural design programs. The low-end programs will allow you to do only very basic designs and the extreme high-end versions will probably be beyond the ability of the average rehabber.

The software that I use retails for about $200 and will do an amazing number of things. You can design and remodel all areas of a house as well as create landscaping plans and decks. You can change paint colors, carpet and tile, cabinet styles, get 3-D views and do a virtual walk-through of the house. It does take a while to learn how to use it effectively but it is well worth the effort. Most software will have built in tutorials to assist you in getting started.

Demolition

After you have planned everything out and established your timeline, as well as engaged contractors where needed, you are ready to begin. I usually start off projects with any demolition and clean out that may be necessary. It is possible to do the demolition room by room as needed, but I prefer to do it all at once. If the demolition work is not too extensive you may be able to do it yourself. If it is a larger project, you can usually hire cheap labor to speed things along. When the demolition is complete, you have a clean slate to work with and are ready for the next step.

Beginning the Renovation

With all of the old material out of the way it's time to start putting in the new. Things need to follow a logical sequence, you don't want to do something and then wind up having to remove it because you should have done something else first. Start with things like plumbing and electrical work, after that is completed, you can move on to insulation.

After all of the rough in of plumbing and electric, along with hanging and finishing drywall, you are ready for the next step. At this point you would begin installing new bathroom fixtures or kitchen cabinets followed by flooring, tile, molding etc.

As you can see, there is a lot to coordinate. When you are dealing with different contractors, you need to manage your timeline effectively. You can hire a project manager if you aren't comfortable handling this yourself, but that would add additional cost and cut into your profit. You need to decide how much of the project to do yourself and how much to contract out. It is possible to be successful without doing any of the work yourself.

There is another possibility that can also work out very well. This is to partner with a contractor. There are many contractors who would love to be involved in rehab projects but lack the money or the knowledge of investing in real estate. If you partner with someone like this, you could wind up doing larger projects with lower construction costs. The trade-off would be giving up a piece of your profits. There are many contractors who will trade their sweat for equity in the project. This route also provides you with someone who is highly motivated to keep costs down and quality up.

Permits

Prior to beginning any work you should check with the local building department. Some of the work may require permits and inspections by the municipality. If you do work without the required permits the job could be stopped and you may be required to remove work that has already been completed. Another problem could arise when you go to sell the house. Trying to cut corners could wind up costing a lot more down the road. While many people find permits and inspections to be an inconvenience, these requirements exist for good reason. The regulations insure that any work meets the local building codes and the inspections assure you that the work is being performed to acceptable standards.

Minor things and cosmetic fixes, such as paint and carpet, do not usually require a permit. Major renovations that include plumbing, electrical work or structural changes usually will require that you pull permits. Many people are tempted to do things without getting the necessary approvals in order to save time or money. This is something that can come back to bite you and end up costing a lot more in the long run. To be sure that the work is done properly and in accordance with the local building codes, the building department will inspect all work and the inspector will have to sign off on it. This can protect you if your contractors are not doing the proper job. If you do work without the proper permits, you may have difficulty when it is time to sell. If a title search finds that work was done without building department approval, you may need to get the permits prior to being able to sell. Getting a permit after the fact can result in fines or penalties and may require that any improper work to be corrected or removed. Trying to save a few dollars by circumventing the process can wind up costing you a lot more in the end.

Basic Systems

The first things that you need to deal with when rehabbing a house are the basic systems. Homebuyers have certain expectations of any property that they are considering. They expect that the plumbing works, the electrical system meets an acceptable standard, the heat works and the roof is adequate. If these basic expectations are not met, then they will usually pass on the house or expect to pay a lot less for it. A lender will also expect that these items meet a sufficient standard in order to approve a mortgage on the property.

If the roof needs minor repairs do not hesitate to do them. If the roof is in poor condition, then it needs to be replaced. You need to check your local building code to see if you can re-roof over the existing shingles or if the old roof needs to be removed. While a new roof may not add a lot to the value of a property, a bad roof can make it extremely difficult to sell. If the roof is in very poor condition the buyers may have difficulty obtaining a mortgage.

The electrical system should be upgraded if necessary. Most older homes were not designed to handle the needs of today's appliances. Upgrading the electrical panel to higher amperage is usually sufficient. In some cases it may be necessary to add additional outlets and fixtures, but it is rare for a house to need to be completely rewired.

Plumbing is another area where buyers have basic expectations. They want to have sufficient water pressure. This can be a problem in some older homes. Septic systems are also a concern; a system with problems needs to be dealt with. If the house is hooked up to a sewer system, you need to be sure that the drainage is good. If not, you may need to have the sewer lines from the house to the street cleaned.

The heating system needs to be functioning properly. If it is an oil-fired system it should be tuned up. If it is a gas system, it should be checked to assure that it is functioning properly. If the system is electric, you may wish to upgrade older units to more efficient ones.

In warmer climates you have air conditioning units to deal with. Has the system been recently serviced? Have the filters been changed and the ducts cleaned?

Repairing the various systems may not add value to the house, but systems in poor condition definitely subtract value. Most buyers will insist on a home inspection. These systems are the first thing that an inspector will look at.

Kitchens

So what should you do to make the house as valuable as possible? It is common knowledge that kitchens and baths are the primary selling points of almost any house, so you should start there. What you do should depend on the other houses in the neighborhood. The ideal situation is for your property to be a little nicer than the competition. What you do not want is for your house to be so good that you are not able to recover your costs. If other houses have cheap laminate cabinets then yours should be a nice oak or maple. If other houses have low-grade wood cabinets then yours should be a nicer grade. If the neighborhood standard seems to be low quality you do not need to blow your budget on high-end cherry cabinets.

Sometimes you can get away with painting the existing cabinets and upgrading the hardware. There is also the possibility of re-facing the old cabinets to make them look new. If the cabinets do not have handles or knobs, you may be able to achieve a much better look by adding them. Older hardware can be upgraded as well; a new set of handles can make an older set of cabinets appear fresh. Instead of automatically ripping everything out, look to see if the existing cabinets can be refreshed.

Countertops can make a big difference. If there is not a lot of counter space, you can achieve a very expensive look without spending a fortune. There are companies that will cover old counter tops with granite or you may wish to use tile where there had been a laminate surface. If it is a house in a lower priced area, you may even be able to get away with prefabricated tops from the local home improvement stores.

In a case where the kitchen is very out-dated, or in poor condition, you may have no choice but to gut it and start over. If that is the case, you have a clean slate to work with and you should plan carefully. This is a time when you should think outside the box. On my first rehab project I was struggling with the kitchen renovation. It seemed that whatever I thought of wouldn't work. I was talking to someone about the problem I was having, and I innocently said that it would be easy if the bathroom wasn't where it was. The person I was talking to said simply "Why don't you move the bathroom?" it was like being hit with a sledgehammer. The solution was so simple, but I couldn't see past the problem. It was a great lesson. When I worked up a plan that included relocating the bathroom to the other side of the kitchen, everything fell into place. This illustrates the benefit of sharing ideas with other people in order to get input from someone who may have a better method of dealing with problems.

If you are replacing cabinets and countertops, you should utilize the kitchen designers at home improvement stores like Lowe's ®and The Home Depot®. The designers can create computerized drawings and layouts of the project. A good designer can point out many things that you might not think of. They are also used to dealing with people who are looking for the latest styles and features available. The designs are usually free but there may be a charge to have the area measured. The measuring fee is usually credited to the purchase of the cabinets. You can supply your own dimensions but I would recommend that you pay for the measuring service in order to avoid costly mistakes.

Having an updated and modern kitchen can have a huge impact on your ability to sell a house at the price that gives you a nice profit. Remember that you are looking for that "wow" factor while staying within your budget.

Bathrooms

The bathroom is another critical room in the house. Older houses had simple but functional bathrooms. They were typically 5'x7' with a tub, toilet and sink. Today you will find oversized whirlpool tubs, separate showers, double sinks, closets and a toilet. The bathroom in a newer house is frequently several times larger than the bathrooms in older houses. If you are doing a total renovation of the bathroom, you should enlarge it if the floor plan allows. You may be able to reconfigure another room, closet or hallway to gain space. As with kitchens, you should upgrade the bathroom so that it is a notch above the competition without going overboard.

If the house is in a higher priced neighborhood, you may want to use granite countertops and shower walls. If it is in a lower priced area, you can use less expensive tub surrounds and cultured marble sink tops. Let the area dictate how extensive the makeover should be. A bathroom, like a kitchen, can have a lot to do with how difficult or easy it is to sell the house. One thing to avoid is using cheap fixtures and faucets in any house. In a high-end area you obviously need to use high-end faucets and fixtures. What you shouldn't do is use low quality in a lower end house. That is not to say that you should use an expensive faucet in a low cost area. What you should use is a medium grade brand name. It is not a lot more expensive than the cheaper alternatives but it looks a lot nicer. You will also encounter fewer problems when installing them and if you need parts for any reason they are easier to get. The difference in price is minimal in comparison to the problems that you can avoid. My experience has been that when I use the cheapest materials things just don't seem to fit right or work like they should.

Lighting

You need to consider your lighting choices when renovating a house. You have many options including recessed lighting, track lighting, fluorescent fixtures and traditional incandescent lighting. The style of the house will dictate your choices. A contemporary style house will have lighting fixtures to match. On older property will have a different style but the fixtures should still be as up to date and efficient as possible. Outdated lighting fixtures make a house look old, so replace them.

Flooring

Flooring is an area that can easily update the look of a house. Start with carpeting. What kind of condition is it in? If it is fairly new and in good shape you can have it cleaned. In most cases with a rehab project it will not be in good shape. When it comes to flooring remember the following adage: when in doubt, rip it out! New carpet is a very cost-effective way of improving the look of a room. Once again the area standard comes into play: be sure the quality of the carpet matches what is expected in the area. The cheapest carpet should be avoided unless the house is going to be a rental. It is not usually necessary to use the most expensive material, but the type of carpet and level of quality can make a big difference in the appearance. The difference in price may only be a few dollars per yard between a low grade and a medium grade carpet. That may translate into a few hundred dollars for higher quality and better looks. That is usually well worth the cost.

Wood floors can add an elegant feel to a house. The look of freshly finished wood can give the property a sense of warmth. In many houses you may find that dingy old carpets are covering nice hardwood floors that can be sanded and stained at a lower cost than replacing the existing carpet. If you come across this situation, you should refinish the floors if at all possible.

Pre-finished wood flooring is great if you are looking to install a new hardwood floor. You eliminate a lot of steps because you do not have to install the floor and then put stain and polyurethane on it. The cost is generally similar but the time you save may be well worth it.

Laminate floors are designed to look like wood but are less expensive and easier to install. This is a project that someone with limited experience can easily tackle. When choosing a laminate flooring system, watch the quality. The cheapest versions look cheap, while the better grades can help you achieve a very nice look.

Seamless vinyl flooring is another popular option. It usually is installed in one piece and is very cost effective. It is popular because it comes in a variety of styles and colors and is easy to clean. It is widely used in low-end to mid range housing. It should be noted that buyers of higher cost houses would generally expect a better quality floor.

Tile floors come in many different types such as ceramic, porcelain, slate and travertine. There are many different sizes of tile and quality varies, as do the prices. The better the house, the better the quality of tile that you should use. Be careful with color and style as well. While a buyer can change paint colors and carpet fairly easily, a tile floor is much more difficult and costly to change.

Landscaping

One area that shouldn't be overlooked is landscaping. Many new rehabbers do not want to spend time and money on the yard. They do not realize the importance of curb appeal. When you are out looking at properties, pay attention to how you react when you see a house for the first time. Chances are that you have already formed an opinion before you have even gone inside, that opinion is curb appeal.

A house that looks good from the outside, and is well landscaped, will have you thinking positive thoughts before you step inside. If you feel good before you walk, in you unconsciously want that feeling to continue. Conversely, a house with poor curb appeal will have you in a bad frame of mind. You will automatically start looking for the negative aspects on the inside.

The exterior of the house needs to look good. You may need to add new siding or fresh paint. If the exterior is brick, you may need to power wash it and repair the mortar where needed. If the exterior is in decent shape, you may wish to add shutters or other accessories to give it a better look. Try stepping back and looking at the house as if you were seeing it for the first time. What can be done to make it look better?

How is the entry door? Should it be changed or painted? Having a front door that stands out in a positive way can have a dramatic effect on the entire house. If there is a screen door or storm door, what kind of shape is it in? If it doesn't look good it should be replaced.

How is the landscaping? If the yard is overgrown, you should get rid of as much as needed to have the yard looking neat. The front of the house should not be concealed by trees and shrubs; a well cared for front yard says a lot about the house.

The back yard should also be in good shape. While it may not be as important as the front yard in terms of curb appeal, it needs to look good. Debris and clutter should be removed from the back yard and the landscaping should look well cared for. A backyard rarely sells a house, but a yard in poor shape can hurt your chances of making a sale.

Problems

So far everything is going according to plan. You've planned every-thing carefully, coordinated all of the work and followed the timeline. Things are going smoothly and suddenly an issue pops up or a prob-lem rears its ugly head. It could be any number of things. Maybe you encountered electrical or plumbing problems, a structural deficiency or a mold issue. Everything comes to a halt and panic sets in. The first thing to remember is that it is virtually impossible to take on this type of project without encountering problems. What you need to do is to evaluate the situation and explore your options. You need to come up with the best possible solution and get the work flowing again. Usually, after the initial panic subsides and you consider the solutions, you will find that the issue isn't as bad as you initially thought. The fact is that it is there, so you need to deal with it as best you can and move on. If you allowed for contingencies in your budget, you should be able to handle most problems that arise. If you really blew it, you just need to do the best that you can.

Mold

A major concern that is getting a lot of media attention is mold. This is something that cannot be ignored. There are many different kinds of mold. Some mold is fairly benign and can be dealt with easily. Other forms of mold, such as black mold, are highly toxic and can be difficult to remove. Many states now have a disclosure requirement for mold much like a lead-based paint disclosure.

If the house has a mold problem, you should not ignore it or try to hide it. If a buyer finds out that you knew about a mold problem and failed to disclose it, you could have a serious liability issue. The best course of action is to have the mold removed by a company that specializes in mold remediation. After they have corrected the problem, they will issue a certificate that states that the house is free of mold. The cost of these services may not be cheap but they are nothing compared to the liability you could face by trying to hide the issue.

Pests

Termites and other pests can be a minor nuisance or a major problem. You should never purchase a home without having a pest inspection. It is usually the seller's responsibility to be sure that the house is termite free prior to sale. If there is significant damage, you can use that as a bargaining chip in your negotiations. If you are using conventional financing, the lender will probably insist on a pest inspection prior to closing the loan. Termites are the most common pests but there are others such as carpenter ants.

Radon

This statement is on the Web site of the U.S. Environmental Protection Agency: *Radon is a cancer-causing natural radioactive gas that you can't see, smell or taste. Its presence in your home can pose a danger to your family's health. Radon is the leading cause of lung cancer among non-smokers.*

Radon enters your home by rising up through the ground and coming in through cracks and holes in the foundation. The gas is then trapped inside the house. A home inspector should test the home for excessive levels of radon. If necessary, steps may be needed to mitigate the problem. Many states certify or license radon contractors and the system used will vary based on the design of the house. Costs can be expected to run from $500 to $2,500 depending on what is needed.

Wrap-up

The end of a project can be the most exciting as well as the most nerve wracking. It seems there are a thousand little details to contend with. The way that you get a handle on all of those details is by creating a *punch-list* of things that need to be done. The list needs to be sorted by priority and arranged by job type. Items should be grouped so that things are done in an orderly and timely manner. For example, you'll want to complete all kitchen tasks at the same time, then move on to another room, and out to the yard until the list is completed. When you are done, you have finished the project and are ready to move on to the next step in the process—the sale.

Summary

Create a Timeline

Decide on Contractors

Get Necessary Permits

Follow a Logical Sequence:

- Basic Systems

- Kitchens & Baths

- Lighting

- Flooring

- Landscaping

- Deal With Problems

- Mold/Pests/Radon

- Punch List

A Rehabber's Tale

Frank

Frank Adams is a veteran real estate investor with thirty years of experience, having owned rental properties in Texas since 1978. A former resident of Houston where he was a manufacturer's rep selling nuts, bolts, tools and other items to industrial distributors, he now lives in the Hill Country of central Texas. Frank took advantage of the housing glut that followed the crash of the oil markets in the early 1980's where he was able to acquire a number of rehab properties at very attractive prices. He now has over 50 projects under his belt.

One of Frank's projects was located about 55 miles west of Austin in the town of Granite Shoals. He purchased the property in April of 2003 for $42,000. This was a fairly typical rehab project for him.

> **Frank:** "I had already purchased four houses from this agent when she called me on this one. It was an 'estate settlement' deal. Husband and wife, in their 80s, had died within hours of each other.
>
> The first time we saw the house there was so much stuff in it you could barely turn around. Much of it was in the process of being priced for the yard sale and the listing agent was surprised that anyone had shown it in its present condition.
>
> This was a 940 square foot +/-, 2 bedroom, 1 bathroom, house. It actually looked like a mobile home but it was stick built. The first thing I noticed was that there was an 8' X 12' laundry room off the master bedroom. This was just crying out to be converted to a ½ bath. The only bathroom was immediately behind the kitchen.
>
> Asking price was about $56K, we offered $38K CASH, with a two week closing. The only thing I wanted was for the seller to treat the termites and have the garage sale. Two days later the agent called back

and said 'the seller is not responding to your offer, but they want you to know they are dropping their asking price to $44K.' I told her to change our offer to $42K and they accepted it 10 minutes later.

At the time, I lived in Houston (200 miles away) but we were getting ready to move 10 miles from this house. I loaded up my car with some basic tools, a trundle bed and some cookware and other kitchen stuff and moved in Mondays through Thursday or Friday for a few weeks. I started out doing some repairs on the exterior, doing some basic painting while my brain worked through the bathroom project."

Frank understands the importance of controlling costs and is a bargain hunter at heart. Keeping the rehab expenses down can have a great impact on the profit that is ultimately realized.

Frank: "I bought a 5 gallon pail of exterior paint at HD (whoops paint) for $15. I had a fair amount of PVC pipe around my place and there was more PVC in the shed at this house. I did have to buy a toilet flange and some joints as well as several cans of PVC primer and cement!

The subdivision where we lived in Houston did not allow yard sales, except once a year, with a permit. As we were preparing to move we participated that year. My wife sold while I rode my bicycle around the neighborhood looking for bathroom fixtures. Here's what I found:
Toilet, with seat:
$5
Matching towel racks, toilet paper holder
and hooks to hang your robe
$3
30" wide cultured marble sink, with Delta faucet.
$Free
(my favorite price)

When looking for a sink base for the top I realized that the combo of base and top would cost less than the base only. So I continued looking. One day my wife told me to come to HD as they had a discontinued 'pedestal' sink for $5. I asked the guy whether it was the base or the sink itself and he looked them up, he said EACH PIECE was $5. 'SOLD' I said. He said he didn't have time to take the display off the pegboard so I told him I would do it."

In the end the project went very well and resulted in a nice profit.

"This rehab went a lot smoother than some that I had done. I didn't find any further problems when I tore things apart and really had no 'surprises' while doing this project.

Cost:

Exterior paint	$15
Interior paint	$25
PVC, PVC cement and other plumbing misc.	$75
Hardie Panels	$75
Yard sale stuff	$8
Door locks, broken window, other miscellaneous	$80
Gas, 8 roundtrips X 400 miles @ 25 MPG	$200
Total	**$500 rounded**

I had a quote for $1700 to re-carpet the floors but the guy couldn't do it for another week. I showed the house with bare floors and sold it to the second couple that looked at it. Their son-in-law was a flooring guy and they wanted him to do it, so I credited the $1700.

I sold it for $62K minus $1700 flooring allowance for a net of $60,300. I financed it with $2K down @8.5%. Buyer's P&I is $448.28.

However, I calculate my income stream on the $40,500 that I've actually got in the deal-purchase price, plus fix up minus down payment. I calculate that I'm earning a cool 13% on my investment.

These guys purchased the house in May of 2003, here we are November 2007 and they've always paid on time."

Frank's business model is to purchase property for cash and rehab them as economically as possible. He then offers them for sale with owner financing and a small down payment. While some may perceive holding mortgages as high risk, Frank has had very few problems with this strategy. What he has done is build a very nice monthly income stream from the mortgage payments. Frank is an excellent example of what you can achieve by rehabbing real estate.

Chapter 10

Making the Sale

The reward of a thing well done is to have done it.
—**Ralph Waldo Emerson**

The rehab is complete and you are ready to sell. Now the real game begins. If you thought buying was fun, wait until you see how nerve-wracking selling can be. There are many variables that will determine how well the sale goes. The most important is the state of the real estate market in the area. If the market is really hot, the only thing you have to worry about is pricing your property so that you don't leave a lot of profit on the table. However, that is not usually the case. In a balanced market, which is one where houses change hands at a steady pace, you need to be concerned about setting a fair price and being sure that the home shows well. If you set the price too high, it probably will sit on the market with the carrying costs eating into your profit a little every day. If you set the price too low, you are giving away your profit. My preference is to be sure that my house is a little bit better than the others on the market and priced at, or below, the recent sales in the neighborhood. In a very slow market you may have to offer a significant discount or other incentives to make your house stand out from the rest and attract a buyer.

Setting the Price

So how do you set the price? If this were the stock market it would be easy, one share of General Motors is exactly the same as another, and the market will tell you the price on any given day. If GM is selling for $25 a share, you will not be able to sell yours for $40. Real estate is different because no two houses are exactly alike. Even in a brand new development where every house is built exactly the same way there are differences due to lot location, upgrades and decorating choices. This makes pricing real estate a mix of art and science. The prices will have a limit however. This is why it is important not to rehab your house to a point where it is too far above the other homes in the neighborhood. If you overdo it, you will have a difficult time recovering your investment.

The most common way to set the value is to research comparable sales in the area. You should compare things such as square footage, number of rooms and bathrooms, lot size, age of the home, proximity to schools and shopping, and any other factors that would make homes similar. You should also give more weight to recent sales since they will more accurately reflect the current state of the market. You also want to look at the asking prices of homes that are currently for sale and how long they have been on the market. If a house has been on the market for a significant period of time that is a good indication that the asking price is too high. Remember that any home will sell if it is priced right. The idea is to price it at a point that will attract a large number of people to look at the home. Watch out for breakpoints as well. When people are looking for a home, they may search for houses that are priced in a certain range. For example, if people are looking for a house with a maximum price of $300,000 and yours is priced at $302,000 it has an excellent chance of being overlooked. A better price may be $299,900 since this will most likely result in the property being viewed by many more people. Statistics show that a significant number of buyers view homes on the internet prior to contacting an agent or seller. When they put a price range into a Web site's search field they tend to do it in certain ranges, so if you are priced above that range you will not be seen.

How do you find comparable sales information? Municipalities record real estate sales and the information is generally a matter of public record. This means that you can obtain the information from your county clerk, recorder or assessor depending on the area that you are in. Many of these agencies have the information available in an on-line database. Real estate agents and appraisers can also provide you with this information, but my preference is to do my own research. That is not to say that I do not ever solicit the opinion of a professional, sometimes their insight and market knowledge can prove to be invaluable.

Agent vs. FSBO

After you have decided on a price, you need to decide how to sell. Do you want to sell it yourself or use an agent? There are pros and cons to each. A lot will depend on your knowledge when it comes to selling real estate and your desire to handle a complicated transaction. The market will also play a role in that decision. If a market is really hot, it may be fairly easy to sell your own home. If the market is fair or slow, it may prove to be very difficult to sell without the help of a professional. I have done it both ways and my preference is to use an experienced agent. The key word here is "experienced," using your Aunt Millie or Cousin Fred who has a license but has never sold a house is probably worse than selling it yourself. Dealing with an inexperienced agent can be difficult as well. Every day that the house sits on the market costs you money, if you are going to use an agent be sure to use a good one.

If you decide to do a For Sale By Owner, or FSBO, be sure to do it with a plan. It usually takes more than sticking a sign on the lawn, even in a hot market. Determine how you are going to market the property, are you going to advertise? There are firms that offer limited services to sellers such as advertising, placement on internet listings, signage, flyers, etc. The fees will usually be substantially less but that doesn't mean that you are getting a better deal. Like anything else, you have to shop around. There is a lot more that goes into selling a house than meets the eye.

The reason my preference is to use an agent is because a seasoned pro that knows the market can be more valuable than any money you might save. Many people react by saying "why should he get 6% for sticking a sign on the lawn?" The truth is that there is a lot more to it than that. An agent can assist you in determining a price, but it should ultimately be your decision since it is your money. An agent will prepare a CMA or Comparative Market Analysis, which will compare your property with others that are on the market as well as with those that have recently sold. This is not to be confused with a professional appraisal, which is concerned mostly with the facts about the property and recent sales. The agent should also prepare a marketing plan, which will show how he intends to sell the house. This plan should include placing the home on the Multiple Listing Service or MLS. A schedule of open houses should be provided as well. Marketing the home through an open house is a great way to get a number of potential buyers to view the house on the same day. The marketing plan could also include advertising the home in newspapers and real estate magazines. The costs of all of these items are the responsibility of the seller's agent. That means that the agent has a vested interest in getting the home sold, if it doesn't sell the agent does not get reimbursed.

The buyer is frequently represented by his own agent. When that happens, the selling agent will split the commission. So you can see that when you break it down the seller's agent isn't making as much as you might think at first. Let's use an example of a house that sells for $200,000, with a 6% commission. At first you might think that the agent who listed the house is pocketing a $12,000 commission upon the sale of the house. In reality it is far less than that. If the commission is split with a buyer's agent, the commission to the seller's agent is down to $6,000. From that amount we need to subtract everything that was spent marketing the property. Advertising, flyers, marketing packages and holding open houses could easily add up to $1,500 bringing the total down to $4,500. The agent must then pay part of that amount with the broker who owns the real estate office that the agent works out of; let's say that amounts to another $1,000. That leaves the agent with $3,500 from which he must also cover the expenses of listings that may have expired without the house being sold. The $12,000 commission that looked so large at first may only be about $3,000 by the time it reaches the agent's pocket. And then let's not forget that the government will have its hand in that pocket looking for its share as well. The point here is to think twice before branding real estate agents as crooks when in fact they are just working to earn a living to feed their families. Nor should we should feel sorry for them, good agents will make a lot of sales and earn a very nice living.

Curb Appeal

So you've decided on whether to use an agent or sell it yourself, now what? An investor will usually look at a deal strictly by the numbers and on the facts. However, the majority of homes are purchased by people who are going to live in them. These buyers tend to act more on emotion. Since that is the case, you need to market to that point of view. First impressions can make or break a sale. For that reason, curb appeal is extremely important. When someone drives up to a house they need to have a good initial reaction. This means that the yard should be clean and the landscaping should be top notch. There should not be any overgrown shrubs or trees and the house should be as presentable as possible. Drive up to the house yourself and look at it as if you were seeing it for the first time, how would you feel about the property if you were in the market for a new home? A house with good curb appeal will have potential buyers feeling good about the property before they even walk through the door.

A word about junk, get rid of it! Junk, debris, clutter, garbage and overgrown yards all cost you money. The visual image that clutter creates can kill a deal. If the garage is packed to the rafters, the potential buyer will get the impression that the house lacks storage space. Like they told you in grade school, neatness counts. If there is no place to put stuff then throw it away, have a yard sale or rent a storage unit. A neat house shows better and a house that shows better, sells better. This applies mainly to houses that you occupy, but a house that was rehabbed and still has a lot of trash lying around is looked at the same way.

Staging

When a potential buyer walks into the house, what do they see? Is it vacant? Many houses are rehabbed and left vacant until they sell. Studies have shown that vacant houses do not sell as well as houses that are occupied. It is harder for people to imagine themselves living in a home that is unfurnished. This is why you will see almost all new homebuilders use furnished models to market their communities. The process of furnishing and decorating a home prior to sale is called staging. Staging the home can result in quicker sales at higher prices. This technique appeals to a buyer's emotions and allows them to imagine themselves living there. There are companies that actually provide home staging services for sellers. If you have a vacant house, that does not mean that you need to go buy furniture and decorative items. Furniture can be rented, as can many of the decorator items that you might need. You can also borrow items from your own home to help with decorating. If the real estate market is really hot, it may not be necessary to go through the trouble and expense of staging the home, but in a normal or slow market it can be well worth it. Remember that ticking clock, every day that the home remains unsold a little more of your profit ticks away. When you are trying to sell a house that is costing you money to keep, time literally is money.

Incentives

What else can you do to help the house sell quickly? You could offer incentives. A good incentive is to give a seller's concession for closing costs. What you actually do is raise the price of the house to cover the cost of the concession. While it looks like you are just playing a game, there is a real benefit to it. Let's go back to the example of the $200,000 house. You could raise the price of the house to $210,000 and give the buyer $10,000 for closing costs. The net cost to you is $0, but there could be a huge benefit to the buyer. Suppose a buyer agrees to the purchase price of $200,000 but only has $45,000 to work with. Closing costs for the mortgage and other title related charges could easily come to $10,000, which only leaves $35,000 for the down payment. Since this is only 17.5% it eliminates a lot of financing options and the buyer can expect to pay a higher interest rate as well as being required to have Private Mortgage Insurance or PMI.

PMI Definition:

Private Mortgage Insurance is insurance provided to lenders by non-government insurers that protects them if the buyer defaults. The insurance premium is paid for by the borrower.

If you were to give a seller's concession of $10,000 for closing costs, the buyer would have the full $45,000 available for the down payment. With a purchase price now set at $210,000 the down payment of $45,000 represents a little more than 21% and allows the buyer to qualify for loan products that do not require the added expense of PMI. Because the risk level of loans rises as the down payment decreases, using a concession to cover closing costs can help buyers at smaller down payment levels to qualify for better programs because money that was going to be used to cover closing costs can now be used to effectively increase the percentage of the down payment. The use of a concession may even allow deals to happen that otherwise wouldn't. There are programs that allow for down payments as small as 5%, so seller paid closing costs may allow a buyer to purchase a house when they otherwise couldn't. It should be noted that while banks allow these concessions to take place, they could be limited. Typically a concession of no more than 3% is allowed with 5% down payments and up to 6% can be allowed with payments of 10% or more. There are other ways around this as well. Some closing items can be designated as being paid by the seller instead of coming from the concession. This is where it pays to have knowledgeable agents, title officers and real estate attorneys.

Seller Financing

Another technique is to offer seller financing. This can actually allow you to sell the house for a higher price. Of course it is easiest if you own the house outright, but it can still work if you don't. If you own the property free and clear, you can ask for a down payment and offer to carry financing at a stated rate of interest, usually a little higher than market rates, for a certain period of time. If you are not inclined to wait 30 years for your money, you could offer to use a 30-year payment schedule but have a balloon payment due in 3 years, 5 years or whatever time you are comfortable with. When the balloon payment is due, the buyer will have to refinance or sell the house to pay you. When you carry back financing you also have the ability to sell that note for cash. You will have to sell it at a discount, but it can still be sold.

But what if you do have a loan on the property? In that case, you can carry a seller second. This means that the buyer obtains a first mortgage for the purchase and you hold a second mortgage for the difference between the first mortgage and the down payment. Let's go back to our $200,000 example. The buyer obtains a conventional mortgage loan for 80% of the purchase or $160,000. He makes a down payment of 10% or $20,000 and you hold a note for $20,000, which is the difference between the down payment and the mortgage that the buyer obtained. What you are really doing is taking a portion of your profit in the form of a note. As in our earlier example, you get to set the interest rate and the length of the loan. This note can be sold as well, but you have to expect that a note buyer will want a bigger discount because it is a second mortgage, not a first, and therefore carries a greater degree of risk. The advantage for the buyer is that he can avoid PMI charges because, as far as the lender is concerned, the primary mortgage is for only 80% of the purchase price.

Lease Option

Another way to move a property is through a *lease-option* or *rent to own* contract. This is a method that can be effective in a slow market. This is also good if you are looking to command a higher price or generate income. There are many people who would like to own a house but are unable to for various reasons. Perhaps they don't have a large enough down payment, maybe they are waiting for their credit to improve or they are not sure that they are going to stay in the area.

A lease option is a rental contract with the option, but not the obligation, to purchase the house for a specific price within a certain time frame. A contract is drawn up that will have a down payment that will be applied to the purchase. A portion of the monthly lease payment is also applied to the down payment. If the sale is not completed the money is forfeited.

The contract will specify a rent payment that is higher than a traditional lease would be on a similar property being used as a rental. An example would be a house that could be listed today at $295,000 or rented for $1500 per month. In the lease option the rent could be $2,000 per month with $750 per month applied towards the down payment. The prospective buyer would also supply a down payment; we'll use $5,500 in this case. They may have a three-year option to purchase for $325,000. If the person leasing the house elects not to buy it they would walk away from the money that they have put in.

Rent = $2,000/month

Credit = $750/month

Down Payment = $5,500

36 month lease/option

36 months x $750 = $27,000

Down payment   = $ 5,500

Total Credit   = $32,500

Purchase Price = $325,000

$32,500 = 10% Down Payment

The advantages for the buyer are that they can accumulate a down payment towards the purchase but are not obligated to buy. If the market has caused home prices to decrease, or if there is another reason why the purchase cannot be completed, the prospective buyer has no further obligation. If the purchase is completed the buyer has accumulated a 10% down payment while renting.

There are many advantages from the seller's point of view as well. The ability to command a higher rental payment may turn a negative monthly cash flow into a positive one. There is also the down payment made at the time of contract. A tenant who intends to purchase the property will usually take better care of the house. There may be a tax benefit to the seller for delaying the sale of the house. A higher price can be set for the house. If the buyer walks away, the seller can pocket the down payment and the additional rent and repeat the process with a new tenant.

The primary disadvantages are that the seller has to wait to receive the money from the sale of the property and any appreciation in excess of the pre-set selling price belongs to the buyer. Despite the drawbacks, a lease-option program can be a great way to sell a house.

Serious Buyers

When selling a house you will have a combination of people who are seriously searching for a home and people who are just out "kicking the tires." It's like going to a department store to buy something or just to window shop. People may just be looking to get a feel for a particular market, or get an idea of what is going on in the neighborhood but are not seriously interested in buying your house or any other. These people will usually walk through quickly and leave. When you hold an open house you will attract many of these window shoppers. It is part of the process so don't let it upset you.

Serious shoppers will tend to spend more time in the house and ask a lot of questions. You may find them going from room to room and back again. They will look at things that someone who is browsing will not. You may find them checking the furnace, looking for signs of leaks or other problems. You will also find them coming back for a second or third look. These are your potential buyers and should be treated as such. You should also look and listen for clues and ask them questions when you have the opportunity.

The more information that you can find out about a buyer, the better chance you have of making a deal. If you can find their underlying motives, you have a much higher likelihood of crafting terms that appeal to the buyer. Just like dealing with a seller, the more information that you have the better. Does the buyer have children? If so, they may need to move at a certain time to accommodate their school schedules. Do they have a home that they need to sell first or do they need to move out of a rental by a certain date? Remember that it's not just the price that matters, the terms of a sale can make a huge difference.

Offers

It's very exciting when your agent calls to tell you that you have an offer. Frequently the excitement of receiving the offer disappears as soon as you hear the terms. Unless you are in an overheated real estate market, the offer will usually be less than what you are asking for the property. Do not despair; this is just the start of the negotiating process.

There are some people out there who make a large number of low-ball offers just to see if one gets accepted. You will have a hard time coming to terms with this type of buyer. When you get one of these you may be better off just rejecting it outright and wait to see if they submit one that is more realistic. If not then you should just move on.

Just because an offer doesn't meet your asking price, it doesn't mean that you can't make a deal. The offer may be loaded with contingencies that make it unacceptable in its present form. Remember receiving an offer doesn't mean that you have a deal; it just means that you may be able to make one.

Negotiating

Negotiating the sale of a home is not much different than when you negotiate to buy. You are on the other side and must watch for contingencies that will allow the buyer to walk away without penalty. Many items that a buyer puts in an offer are just there in order to have something to give away when negotiating. Just as negotiating to buy, be sure to get something in return for every point that you concede. This way you are conditioning the buyer to expect that he will have to give something up for every item he tries to get from you. As you develop better negotiating skills, you will be able to make better deals both when you buy and when you sell.

Sometimes you may receive an offer with a large number of contingencies built in. Frequently the only reason that they are there is so the buyer can use them as bargaining chips during negotiations. To gain the upper hand in the negotiating process the best strategy may be to reject them all at the outset. You could make a very small concession on the price while eliminating all contingencies. This way the buyer will need to negotiate to get the ones that are important to him back in. Each time you concede a point you need to be sure to get something in return.

There may be times when you will not be able to reach an agreement and you have to walk away. Usually if there is a deal to be made, the buyer and seller will find a way to make it happen. The negotiating process is just a way for the buyer and seller to test each other to see where the other's bottom line really is.

Escrow

When it comes to selling a house, the escrow portion of the transaction is much the same as when buying, you are just on the opposite side of the table. The title company and escrow officer will handle the transaction. Some states may have a real estate attorney taking care of the contract and closing. You will be called upon to make decisions throughout the process but the selling side is usually a little easier since you are not dealing with loans or arranging inspections. That doesn't mean that it is smooth sailing, there will always be issues that arise.

It is not unusual for the buyer to seek additional concessions during the escrow process. This will generally happen after an inspection has been performed. Problems may have been uncovered that neither side was aware of. Whether or not you give additional concessions really depends on what problems were revealed and how the negotiating process has gone to that point. By this time the buyer usually has mentally moved into the house and would be seriously disappointed if the deal didn't close. Unless there was a major unexpected problem I wouldn't be inclined to concede much, if anything, at this stage of the game. If you hold firm, the deal will probably close as expected.

Closing

The negotiations are over, inspections have been completed and last minute problems have been solved. It is now time to close escrow. Prior to signing the closing documents and completing the deal, the buyer will usually do a final walk-through of the property. This is generally done to assure the buyer that nothing has happened to the property and everything is as expected. The buyer may wish to verify that any appliances or other items are left as agreed.

When the walk-through is completed and there are no further issues, the closing will proceed. The buyers and sellers each have documents to be signed. There can be problems at this point if the documents contain language that was not agreed to or if conditions haven't been met. These problems can be avoided by being careful prior to the closing date. If each side performs as expected this part of the transaction should go smoothly.

Party Time

At this point you should be counting your profits. In rehab you make your money when you buy by getting the right property at the right price. However, you realize your profit when you sell. This is the time to look back on the deal and see how you did as compared to how you expected to do. You should evaluate what went right and what went wrong. You can learn from your successes and your failures. By critiquing each deal you can help make the next one better. I find it useful to keep a journal of each project. It doesn't need to be elaborate, but it can be very useful going forward. I like to document what was done each day in simple terms. I might put the date and the simple phrase like "gutted bedroom" or "installed kitchen cabinets." The journal is a good memory jog to help you recall specifics of the job. Another thing to do is to take numerous before and after photographs. This can be a great way to help you remember just how well you've done. You can use this to create a portfolio of houses that you've rehabbed. This portfolio can be helpful if you are looking for investors or trying to get funding from your local bank. Having a track record that you can prove is a major asset for your business.

When everything is done, you should be sure to celebrate your success in some way. You may take a nice vacation, simply have a nice dinner or take a few days off. You've worked hard and earned the reward. If you don't reward yourself you might start finding this to be a hard job instead of a rewarding business. Are you ready to do it again?

Summary

Setting the Price

Agent vs. FSBO

Curb Appeal

Staging

Incentives

Seller Financing

Lease Option

Offers

Negotiation

Escrow/Closing

A Rehabber's Tale

Tamara

Tamara Bostrom (pokerbabe78@gmail.com) is a veteran rehabber from the Los Angeles, California area who now resides in Las Vegas, Nevada. Prior to rehabbing homes she had been a marketing consultant and is currently a semi-professional poker player. The southern California market had become extremely expensive, making the holding costs on rehab projects prohibitive. Her frequent trips to the poker tables of Las Vegas eventually drew her to the real estate market there. While the Las Vegas market had also been experiencing very strong appreciation, the cost of entry was significantly lower than the California markets she had been working in.

Interestingly enough, it was her poker playing that initially drew her to real estate:

> **Tamara:** "I was looking for a way to make money that did not involve normal employment. As a poker player, I am acutely aware of the power of leverage. At the card table you use the chips you have in front of you to amass more chips from other players. The concept of leverage at the poker table dictates that you should use as few of your chips as possible (i.e.: make the bet as small as possible) and still have the desired effect. You should leverage your chips. Less is more. So in looking for a new wealth building avenue to pursue, I was attracted to real estate because of all the financial opportunities I considered, it provided the greatest amount of leverage."

The Las Vegas market had slowed considerably by the spring of 2007 and there were many opportunities to be found. One of Tamara's real estate agents had located a bank-owned property that was a perfect rehab candidate. She was able to purchase the property using conventional financing for about 75% of its anticipated market value, which was approximately $265,000. Not having to use hard money financing made the likelihood of a profit much greater.

Tamara acts as her own project manager on her rehab projects. She coordinates and oversees the contractors that she hires in order to be sure that the work is completed to her satisfaction. She is also very good at controlling her costs and sticking to her budget. According to Tamara this project was a "massive remodel including removing two sets of walls to expand the family room and the kitchen. New bathrooms, completely new kitchen, new carpets, new paint, new fixtures, new landscaping front and back." She was able to accomplish all of this while spending only $12,500.

However, the project was not without its share of problems:

> **Tamara:** "We removed a water pipe from the garage that we thought was superfluous only to find out that it was a circuitous route of getting water to the house. We had to reconnect it. After the project was completed, the house was broken into by a large group of teenagers and young adults and used as a party house. The police were called. The neighbors told me about it when I stopped by the next day. The property was vandalized but fortunately the damages were able to be mostly repaired for around $500."

During the time the house was being renovated the market turned sharply downward. Even market veterans can be caught by surprise.

> **Tamara:** "I bought this house as strictly a fix and flip. The renovations went according to schedule and without major incident. We finished on time, but the market took a rather drastic turn for the worse during the course of the rehab ... which was only 9 weeks. When I placed the house back on the market, other homes in the neighborhood had started cutting

their prices to try to sell. My house was remodeled to the top of the neighborhood's standards ... which is where I like to be. I decided that selling the house for less money was not my best option and that my best interests were served by holding the house until the market improved. The frozen capital was not an issue since I am not looking to do anymore projects in the area until the market improves and I had other capital sources available. From the time I started to the time I finished the market completely tanked."

There are many lessons to be learned when things don't go as expected. Experienced investors understand that this is all a part of the process and seek to learn from the difficulty that they experience. If she had a crystal ball to tell her that the market would turn so suddenly she says, "I would have built in more hold time costs in anticipation of possible market decline mid-project."

Tamara: "Always have a backup plan for your back up plan. Have more than one exit strategy. Prepare ahead of time for what you will do if you cannot sell your property in the time frame you anticipate or for the price you want. Will you rent it out and hold onto it until conditions improve? Will you be willing to drop the price and if so, how much? Will you be able to refinance in order to free up capital and then hold the property as a rental? Always consider these alternatives before you buy and leave yourself as many exit strategies as possible."

The steely nerves that are required to be a successful poker player come in handy in real estate as well. Knowing when to hold and knowing when to fold is definitely required in any investment. Tamara has already had a lot of success in rehabbing real estate but there is certainly much more to come.

Part II

The Business of Rehab

Chapter 11

The Business Plan

You've got to be very careful if you don't know where you are going, because you might not get there.—**Yogi Berra**

Do you need a business plan? Many people jump into ventures with no clearly defined plan. When you do not have a plan it is very difficult to assess where you are or how you are doing. It is difficult to make course corrections if you do not know what the course is or when you stray off it. Not only will it be difficult to achieve success without a plan but it will be virtually impossible to claim success if you haven't even defined it.

You may have a general idea of where you want to go and do not feel that you need an actual plan. A pilot may know how to get from New York to Chicago but he will still consult maps and file a flight plan. Being in business is no different, even if you have an idea of where you want to go, it is still better to have a plan. Just as a pilot will consult his compass and other instruments, you can use your plan to be sure that you are on the correct path to your destination.

Do you need a formal business plan? Or will a basic set of business goals that you would like to achieve be sufficient? The answer is that it depends of what your vision for your business is. If your idea is to buy a house, have some fun fixing it up, and make a little bit of profit along the way, then you do not need a fancy business plan. On the other hand, if you want to have a real business making some serious money then you should spend some time and energy on creating a viable business plan. It has been said that people don't plan to fail, they fail to plan. The average person will spend more time planning a summer vacation than they will planning their future.

The elements that a good business plan should include, but need not be limited to, are the following:

- Mission Statement
- Executive Summary
- Objective
- Goals
- Market Analysis
- Strategy
- Implementation
- Financials

Mission Statement

The *Mission Statement* is the overall vision of the company and what they are trying to achieve. The mission statement should be short and to the point. The idea is to convey the mission of the company in a clear and easily understandable manner. An example would be the mission statement for my company:

Rebuilding the American Dream

While simple, it is easily understood. The "American Dream" is to own a home and "rebuilding" is just an indication of rehabbing or rebuilding that home. The mission statement should not be some saying that you frame and hang on the wall; it should be something that defines the mission of your company. The words in your mission statement are truly words to live by.

Executive Summary

The *Executive Summary* is a definition of the structure of the company, the people involved and their positions and responsibilities. The more people that are involved, the more extensive this section will be. If it is only one person, or a husband and wife, it can be very short. If there will be partners involved, then the role of each should be clearly defined in as much detail as possible. The benefit of doing this is that there are fewer opportunities for disputes or misunderstandings if all of the expectations are specified up front.

This section will also detail the type of company such as a C-Corporation, S-Corporation, Limited Liability Company (LLC), Sole Proprietorship, Partnership, etc. The company officers will be listed as well. The larger the organization the more detailed this section will need to be. In a larger company you may wish to create a flow chart detailing who is responsible for what and who people report to.

Objectives

What are the *Objectives* of the company? Is it to strictly rehab houses? Will they be held for rental? Are the properties to be sold immediately upon completion? Perhaps it will be some combination. How big does the company intend to get? All of this should be spelled out in the objectives section.

Goals

One of the most important sections would be *Goals*. Just as you need to set personal goals, your business plan needs to have a set of clearly defined goals as well. They should be as specific as possible and they should include short-term, medium and long-range targets. The goals in the business plan will need to be adjusted on a regular basis as the business progresses.

As you track your progress, you can see how you are actually doing in relation to the goals that you set. If you seem to be missing your target, you may need to reassess your strategy and see why things are not going as you planned. Were the goals unrealistic or is there a flaw in your strategy? Measuring the progress that you are making towards your goals is a great way to give your business a periodic check-up.

Market Analysis

The next aspect of your business plan is the *Market Analysis*. This is where you actually assess the opportunities available in your chosen area. What is the local real estate market like? How many rehab opportunities are there? What is the pricing? Is the market appreciating, depreciating or neutral? Are there a lot of rehabbers to compete with? What are the prospects for the next year, two years, five years, and beyond? Is the profit potential sufficient to justify the risk?

Analyzing your market takes work. You will need to research the sales statistics in the area you are working in. You will also need to physically look at a large number of properties in order to get a handle on the local values. The stock market and commodities markets are relatively easy to analyze in terms of value. The price of a stock or commodity is constantly being set and reset by the markets. One share of a specific stock is exactly the same as another, but no two houses are exactly alike.

Strategy

Now we need to consider *Strategy*. How are you going to achieve the goals that you have outlined? How will you locate the properties to rehab? Will you use birddogs, wholesalers, real estate agents or a combination? What about the rehab work itself? Will you do some or all of it yourself? Will you hire out all of the work? Will it be a combination? If so, what will you do and what will you contract out? Will you be renting the properties or selling them? What is your exit strategy? What is your fall-back position if things don't go as expected?

Implementation

The next step is *Implementation*. This is where you take the strategy and put it into action. When will you begin? What area will you start in? What will your first project be? This is the point at which you put all of this planning into action. Without action your plan is nothing more than a wish.

Financials

The final step is perhaps the most important, *Financials*. The reason that most businesses fail within the first five years is due to insufficient finances. This part is crucial to your business. Many people get started in real estate investing and rehabbing without really understanding the financial aspect of the business. Sure, they investigate mortgages and loans for rehabbing the property, but they ignore the overall finances of the business. They also tend to overlook key aspects of their own personal finances.

Your financial plan needs to include some basic financial assumptions when it comes to how much money you will need and how you will spend it. You need to do a break-even analysis to determine how much you need to make before you turn a profit. You need to have a budget to work from and have a cash flow projection and balance sheet.

Software

There are a number of software programs that can help you complete a business plan. These programs vary in price and sophistication but you can probably start with a very basic program. The program will give you a template to follow where you can simply fill in the blanks as you go along. In the end, you will have a basic business plan. You can then refine this plan as your business grows and you gain a greater understanding of what obstacles or challenges you may face. If you grow large enough, you may reach a point where you wish to obtain bank financing for projects or expansion and the bank will ask to see your business plan. When you reach this point you may wish to hire a professional to create a business plan that will increase your chances of getting a favorable response from a bank.

Your Business Team

Just like a sports team, you need to have a number of players on your business team. Ideally you will all be working together to achieve your respective goals. Each member of the team stands to gain from the relationships and each should be looking out for the best interests of the other. If you assemble a team and find that one of the members is not a good fit, you need to replace them with someone who is. A team that works well together will be a benefit to all. So who do you need on your team?

Accountant

Your first reaction may be that you don't need an accountant until you are making money or you are ready to file a tax return. Nothing could be further from the truth. Rehabbing real estate is a business like any other and needs to be treated as such. When it comes to taxes, it is better to be proactive rather than reactive. An accountant who understands real estate can be a great help here. They can help you set up a system for keeping your tax records and save you a lot of money and aggravation at tax time. The accountant that you choose should have a good understanding of real estate investing and, ideally, be a real estate investor as well.

Attorney

Another key member of your team is the attorney. There are many legal matters involved in real estate investing. A mistake could literally cost you tens of thousands of dollars. It is important to have an attorney who is well versed in the real estate laws of your state. In some states, an attorney will handle the bulk of real estate transactions, while in others a title company will handle most things. If a title company is doing the bulk of the transaction, you still need an attorney to review contracts and draft agreements. You should also use an attorney to handle the formation of your business entity. It is very easy to establish a corporation or LLC on-line, but you run the risk of making significant mistakes that could cost you dearly.

Real Estate Agent

A good real estate agent that truly understands real estate investing is priceless. There are so many agents out there, yet very few of them truly understand what is involved when it comes to investing and rehabbing. Most agents are transaction oriented and are just looking to sell the next house. An investment-oriented agent can help you find deals in any market. If you build a strong relationship with such an agent, you will benefit from their services even when you don't use them. I find many deals without agents, yet they will still supply me with comps and other information that I need because of our relationship. They know that they may not get this deal, but they may get the next one. They also know that if they spot a truly good deal and bring it to me, I may act on it. I will also refer business to them whenever possible.

Lender

A great deal doesn't mean much if you can't find the money to buy it. A good lender knows how to get difficult deals done. There are so many different loan programs and different ways to structure deals. A lender who specializes in doing investor loans will know what the underwriters are looking for and will submit loan applications that have the best chance of getting approved. A professional will also know when they can't make a deal happen and may suggest alternate funding methods. A good lender can save many deals that might not happen otherwise.

Home Inspector

A team member that you will use a lot is a home inspector. By using the same inspector for the majority of your purchases he will learn what you look for. He can help you spot problems that you might miss and save you from making costly mistakes. The inspector will also be furnishing you with reports that can aid in your negotiations with the seller. You will learn the value of a good inspector the first time he stops you from making a bad deal that you were ready to pull the trigger on.

Appraiser

Not to be confused with a home inspector, an *appraiser* is the professional who will set the value on a property. The appraiser will look at the property to determine its size, features and condition. Then they will compare the property to recent sales of similar properties to determine the appraised value. The lender will then use this figure to decide how much of a mortgage they are willing to give. The lender will generally choose which appraiser to use; they want to be sure that they get an impartial assessment of value prior to making a loan. An appraisal is not the same as a comparative market analysis, or CMA, prepared by a real estate agent. The CMA will use recent sales as well as current listings to determine a competitive market price, while an appraiser will only look at actual sales to determine their valuation. You may wonder why you need an appraiser if the bank is the one that selects and hires them. The answer is that there may be times when you want your own appraisal to determine what a good offer would be, and other times that you will need one for reasons other than a loan. One reason may be that you have an option to buy or sell a property based on appraised value or you are using an appraisal to eliminate the need for private mortgage insurance, PMI, on a property you already own. PMI can be dropped once you have a certain amount of equity in a property and an appraisal is used to make that determination.

Escrow Officer

Using the same title company and escrow officer on all of your transactions can make life so much easier. You develop a relationship that shows its true value when problems arise. You become more than just a name on a piece of paper and they will go out of their way to take care of you. I use the same company for almost all of my transactions and they seem to get easier every time.

Insurance Agent

Insurance is one of those absolutely essential items that everyone hates. With so many different companies and policies available it is important that you work with someone who knows the business. Every insurance company seems to have its own niche, what's good in one case is not great in another. There is so much money on the line in real estate that it is extremely important to have the proper coverage. Rehab has its own unique problems in that most companies do not want to write a policy on a vacant property. A good agent who deals with many different companies can help you sort through the maze of confusion.

Contractors

In rehab you definitely need contractors. Even if your plan is to do the work yourself, you still need contractors on your team. You need an electrician, plumber, roofer, handyman and HVAC technician. Even though you may not use them on every job, you need to have people you can rely on. When doing your own work you may encounter times when it makes more sense to contract the work out. Perhaps there is a problem that you can't handle or you have a limited amount of time to complete a project. You will also need contractors to provide you with estimates so that you can evaluate deals. When you work with a contractor on a regular basis, they come to understand your needs and expectations and can help you get things done.

Managing Your Team

Having a strong team can have a huge impact on your business. This is not a place to be bringing your buddies or relatives on board; this is where you want committed people who can have an impact on your success. If you find that a member of your team doesn't meet your expectations you need to find a new team member to replace him. It is important to stay in contact with your team even when nothing is going on. That doesn't mean that you need to talk to them every day, but you should grab lunch or coffee or just chat periodically to be sure that everyone is still in the game. Your team members all have other things going on and are not depending on you to make a living unless you are a huge operation, so it is important to keep in touch so that they are there when you need them.

Summary

Create a Business Plan:

- Mission Statement

- Executive Summary

- Objectives

- Goals

- Market Analysis

- Strategy

- Implementation

- Financials

Assemble a Business Team:

- Accountant

- Attorney

- Real Estate Agent

- Lender

- Home Inspector

- Appraiser

- Escrow Officer

- Contractor

A Rehabber's Tale

Connie Brzowski

Connie Brzowski (http://www.conniebrz.com) is a real estate investor and rehabber from east Texas. She had worked as a labor and delivery nurse until she had children of her own. As her kids got older she
looked for ways to work from home and she eventually started a business performing background checks for non-profit organizations and
small businesses. When this venture didn't pan out as she had hoped,
she and her husband, Buddy, tried their hand at real estate.

They quickly discovered that it was very difficult to find rental
properties that would provide a positive cash flow. However, they also
found that buying properties with the intent of rehabbing them was
something that they could do profitably.

> **Connie:** "It became clear pretty quickly that we could
> negotiate deeply discounted prices on homes with
> years of deferred maintenance—and the rattier the
> house looked, the better the deals we found. Of course
> the trick at that point was learning how much repairs
> and holding costs would add to the price."

Their most recent project is a bank-owned property that they found
in a semi-rural area of Chambers County, Texas. The area has been
enjoying a steady rate of appreciation but didn't experience the boom
that many parts of the country recently had. The bank was asking
$29,000 for the property but they were able to negotiate a final sale
price of $25,500, all cash. They closed the deal in June of 2007.

> **Connie:** "The neighborhood is semi-restricted—lots
> are ½–1 acre each with mature hardwoods—one home
> per lot, one large horse or cow and as many goats and
> chickens as you want. The homes are a mix of nice
> brick homes sitting next to ratty trailers. Half-acre lots

> sell for 25K. The neighborhood has its own water and
> sewer services, which is a big plus in this area and is
> located in the favored school district in the area.
>
> Actually, we were compulsively stalking the vacant
> house next door. For two years, we'd kept an eye on
> an ugly brick ranch waiting for the price to drop out
> of the stratosphere. One afternoon, we noticed a pink
> slip of paper on the door of this horrid little run-
> down shack. When we got home, I checked the MLS
> and found the house—the asking price was only 29K
> so we called our agent."

The house needed quite a bit of work. The exterior needed a new roof, siding windows and a garage door. The interior required some plumbing upgrades, a bathroom renovation and an update to the kitchen including all new appliances. The rest of the house received all new doors, trim needed to be repaired or replaced; crown molding was added to the bedrooms, which also needed new sheetrock on the ceilings. Ceramic floors were installed throughout the house and a fresh coat of paint was added inside and out.

The landscaping wasn't to be ignored either. Overgrown shrubs were removed and debris was cleaned up. Three large trees that had been destroyed by Hurricane Rita had to be cut up and burned in place. The driveway received three loads of crushed rock and a new mailbox was added as a finishing touch.

On their previous projects Connie and Buddy had done the majority of the work themselves. This time they used contractors for most of the work.

> **Connie:** "About a year ago, we realized we were finally
> ready to take our business to a new level—hiring out
> the work rather than doing everything ourselves. We
> started looking for a larger project and when we found
> the Magnolia house, it seemed like the right place at
> the right time for the right price."

This project was not without its share of problems starting with the purchase itself.

> **Connie:** "We had a snafu at the bank during the offer/counter offer which probably cost us several thousand. The bank that owned the property required proof of funds with all offers. Unfortunately, our contact at the bank was having a bad day and refused to provide the letter saying 'it wasn't standard practice.' After lots of aggravation, I finally faxed a copy of our bank balance—a move, which I believe cost us during negotiations and has caused us to reconsider using the local bank. After an offer, counteroffer and counter-counteroffer, we signed a contract and closed two weeks later."

The purchase wasn't the only problem. Mother Nature as well as some design choices caused some difficulty as well.

> **Connie:** "Rain delays! Three full months, waiting for the sky to clear. Because the roof was in such bad shape, we had to wait on all interior repairs until all exterior work was finished.
>
> Early on we decided to use peel-n-stick tile and vinyl plank flooring to save money. Buddy tiled the utility room and bathroom and 3 days later decided to change to ceramic tile flooring. The tiles just weren't sticking well—probably because the weather's cool and damp. For a rental, ceramic tile is a great choice, but we lost time and money making the change midstream."

Connie and Buddy have taken the next step in their business. They've come to realize the value of having a good team and now understand that the "do it yourself" method isn't always the best or most cost effective.

Connie: "This was our first hands-off house. It took time to get used to being the boss and trusting the foreman to do his job. There's no way we could've done this project without a good working relationship with a contractor we trust. That relationship was established two years before this project. Also, we'd already worked with the ceramic tile, laminate and cabinet subcontractors. I doubt we would've taken on a project like this otherwise."

The total cost to rehab the house was just over $33,000 including the holding costs. Adding in the purchase price of $25,500, the final cost of the project was a little more than $58,500. So how did they do? Not too bad!

Connie: "We're keeping this house as a rental. Our real estate agent tells us it could sell for $100K easy and will appraise for $110–115K. We won't be getting an appraisal until we either refinance or take out a HELOC. The house will rent for $850/month."

This was an outstanding project as either a rental or a flip. Connie and Buddy have a very bright future ahead of them in their rehab business.

Chapter 12

Business Structure

The jury consists of twelve persons chosen to decide who has the better lawyer.—**Robert Frost**

Rehabbing homes is a business and as such it has to have the proper structure. There are many forms that this can take and there is no "one size fits all" solution. The proper form depends on your business goals and your current situation. You need to choose between being a sole proprietor, partnership, S-Corporation, C-Corporation, Limited Liability Company (LLC), Limited Liability Partnership (LLP), or Limited Partnership.

If it seems complicated that's because it is. The structure that you choose can have a profound impact on your liability and tax situation. While I will attempt to briefly explain each entity, there is no substitute for using a qualified professional to help you choose the business structure that makes the most sense for you. Trying to save a few dollars by doing it yourself, could wind up costing you much more in the long run.

Sole Proprietor

When many people start out they do not think of structuring their business in any certain way, they just buy a property and start knocking down walls. Everything is in their name and any gains are simply reported on their personal tax return. By default, they are a *sole proprietor*. This may not make a big difference when it comes to taxes but their personal assets are at risk when it comes to liability. If you have liability insurance and are not in a situation where you have a major liability risk, then this set-up may be sufficient. If you are going to be holding properties as rentals or if you are hiring unlicensed or uninsured contractors, you may wish to consider another entity that can help protect your personal assets against liability claims.

If you do not have a significant amount of personal assets, you might assume that you do not have to worry about liability claims. This is not the case. If you were to lose a lawsuit you could have a judgment placed against you that results in the loss of future earnings or assets. If the claim is small you might have homeowners or umbrella liability that would cover it, but a larger claim could be a problem.

From a tax perspective, a sole proprietorship is not usually the most advantageous structure. Any ordinary income is subject to self-employment tax. This tax is currently 15.3% until a threshold is reached at which the rate is dropped to 2.9%, which is the Medicare portion of the tax. This threshold amount increases each year and was $97,500 in 2007.

Partnership

If you are in business with someone other than your spouse, you might set up a *partnership*. A partnership can have two or more people and the partnership agreement defines the percentage that is owned by each partner. This can be a benefit when it comes to taxation since the percentage of ownership will dictate each partner's share of the profits. This may not be the best option in terms of liability protection. If you have a partnership and a business related liability results in a claim against one partner it could result in the assets of the other partners being exposed to the claim as well. You may have liability insurance, but if the loss limits are not high enough to cover the claim the partners can be held responsible for the excess. If a partner makes a mistake that you had absolutely nothing to do with you might find yourself losing your personal assets anyway.

S-Corporation

Some people will choose a corporate structure for their business. One such structure is an *S-Corporation*. The "S" stands for small, it will have no more than 100 shareholders and can have as few as one. The shareholders must be citizens or legal residents of the United States. An S-Corp will provide liability protection and the profits and losses will flow through to the shareholders. The S-Corp must file its own tax return and profits are reported on form K-1 which the shareholder uses to show profit or loss on their individual tax return.

S-Corps offer taxation similar to a partnership but offer superior liability protection. The S-Corp can help avoid some self-employment tax as well. Any income that is considered to be profit would not be subject to FICA or self-employment taxes. The shareholders of the corporation do have to pay themselves a salary that is commensurate with the amount of work that they perform. That salary is subject to FICA taxes. Your accountant can help you determine what the proper amount of salary is.

An S-Corp is considered the preferred entity if you are going to be flipping a large number of properties due to the ability to avoid some of the self-employment tax. It is not considered the preferred method of owning rental properties due to rules regarding the treatment of passive income, such as rental income.

C-Corporation

The *C-Corporation* has certain advantages over the S-Corp in that you can choose your year-end to be other than December 31st. The main disadvantage is that this entity could result in double taxation. The profits are taxed to the corporation and then taxed again as they are passed on to the shareholders in the form of dividends. Other disadvantages are the potential for accumulated earnings tax and the fact that tax rates for the corporation can be higher than personal rates. This is an entity that is seldom used for real estate investments.

Limited Liability Company

One of the most popular entities today is the *Limited Liability Company* or LLC and, to a lesser extent, the *Limited Liability Partnership* or LLP. The primary reason for the popularity of the LLC is that it is a highly flexible entity where you can receive the protection of a corporation with the tax simplicity found in sole proprietorships and partnerships. The earnings from the LLC pass through and are reported on the individual tax returns of the LLC members. The liability protection means that creditors can only go after the assets of the LLC, not the assets of the individual members.

Some advisors recommend having one LLC for each investment property while others suggest having multiple properties in an LLC. If you have multiple properties in one LLC, you need to understand that the combined equity of the properties is at risk in the event of a liability claim. Therefore you should be aware of how much is at risk and set up a new LLC when you feel the need to spread the risk around.

The Corporate Veil

The corporate veil is a legal protection that applies to shareholders, or members in the case of an LLC, that protects their personal assets from creditor claims against the corporation or LLC (the entity). However, in a legal proceeding against the entity, one of the first things the attorney for the plaintiff (the person who initiates a lawsuit) will do is attempt to pierce or lift the corporate veil. If he is successful, then the shareholders or members can be held personally liable.

How could the veil be pierced? If the entity was not properly structured or if correct procedures were not followed the veil could be lifted. This frequently happens when someone does a do-it-yourself entity formation in an attempt to save money and acts as if the entity's assets were his own. There are some formalities that need to be followed and they vary by state. Directors may need to be appointed, officers elected, shares of stock issued and annual meetings held. Financial records need to be kept and an operating agreement and by-laws may need to be in place. Some common things that may cause the veil to be pierced are the co-mingling of funds (using corporate funds for personal use), or outright fraud. If a court determines that an entity was set up with the intent of using it for fraudulent purposes and avoiding liability then the veil will almost definitely be lifted.

I strongly urge people to use professionals to set up their entities in order to avoid these problems. Once everything is properly set up and you understand the correct procedures to follow you can revert to a do-it-yourself mode if you prefer.

Limited Partnership

A *limited partnership* is an entity that is used to protect the investors, or limited partners, from liability. In addition to limited liability, these partners generally are limited in terms of decision making as well. These entities are generally formed when a project is looking for investors to fund it. There will be one or more general partners and a number of limited partners. The liability protection extends only to the limited partners; the general partners are exposed to liability claims. This is not an entity that is commonly used for rehab properties.

Equity Sharing

Another business arrangement that can be used with any business entity is an equity sharing agreement. This is an arrangement that became more common when real estate became extremely expensive in markets such as Los Angeles and New York. A common set-up often exists between a parent and a child. Let's say, for example, that a son or daughter was the buyer and had the income to support the payment but lacked the down payment that was needed. The parent might provide the money needed for the down payment and an equity sharing agreement might be drawn up that spelled out the percentage of ownership and the other terms of the arrangement. After a period of time, the property might be sold or refinanced. At that time, the down payment would be returned and the price appreciation would be split according to the terms of the agreement. If the split was 50/50 the appreciation would be shared equally between the two parties.

Purchase Price = $500,000

Down Payment @ 20% = $100,000

Term of agreement = 5 years

Party A provides down payment of $100,000

Party B obtains mortgage of $400,000

House is sold after 5 years for $700,000 net

Party A receives $100,000 for return of down payment Party B receives mortgage principal pay down

Equity to be Shared = $200,000

The above example shows the purchase of a house for $500,000 with a down payment of 20% or $100,000. After five years, the house is sold and the proceeds distributed. The parent who put up the $100,000 down payment receives it back when the house is sold. Any payments of principal by the son or daughter are paid to them. The appreciation amounted to $200,000 and was split 50/50 between the parent and son or daughter. The child now has $100,000 to buy his next house and the parent received $100,000 for making the investment. In this example, that amounted to an annual return of almost 15%.

While these agreements started in order for parents to help their children, they evolved into investment opportunities for many people. Agreements were made between people who shared a house as well as between people who purchased houses as investment properties. The advent of stated income and low documentation loans has seen these arrangements decrease in recent years. However, the tightening of lending standards may result in equity sharing regaining its popularity.

Insurance

While it's great to have various entities to protect us from liability, there is no substitute for being properly insured. With insurance you are trading a known (insurance premium) for an unknown (risk). By paying a small amount of money, you are transferring a much larger risk to an insurance company.

Insurance companies use the law of large numbers to assess how much they will need to pay out in claims. From that they can determine how much they need to charge in premiums to cover those claims and to provide for their desired profit. They are able to use history and the law of averages to determine how big their risk is. Hypothetically, they are able to accurately predict that if they insure 1,000 people they will have 25 claims. Those claims will cost them a predictable amount of money. What they don't know is who will suffer those claims. Insurance companies will use all sorts of information to minimize their exposure to risk in their underwriting process and reject those applicants that they perceive to be an unacceptable risk.

You may never have a fire but do you want to assume the risk by not being insured? Everyone hates paying insurance premiums until they have a claim. It is a necessary tool to help you keep your exposure to risk manageable. You can reduce your premiums by carrying a higher deductible but you should not skimp on the quality of coverage to save a few dollars. I also recommend carrying the maximum dollar amount of liability coverage that you can get.

Umbrella Liability

An *Umbrella Liability* policy is one that will step in and protect you when you have exhausted the coverage on your regular insurance policies. If you have a limit on your automobile policy of $500,000 but are hit with a $1,000,000 claim you are on the hook for $500,000 and stand to lose other assets. If you have an umbrella liability policy the insurance company will step in to pay the excess.

Most insurance agents will tell you that in order to get an umbrella liability policy you must have your homeowners and automobile policies with the same company. In many cases they are correct; the companies that they work with will not provide coverage unless they have all of your business. If it makes sense for you to do so, there is nothing wrong with using one company for all of your coverage. However, there are a number of companies that will issue stand-alone umbrella liability policies. You can expect to pay higher rates in this case but this insurance is too important not to have.

Do Your Homework

This was just a brief explanation of the different ways that you can structure a business. There is no perfect solution; you need to find the way that works best for you. Everyone has different needs and unique circumstances, what is right for one person may be totally wrong for the next. You need to assess your business goals and see what works best for you both long-term and short-term. A consultation with tax and legal professionals can help you find the best solution for you.

Summary

Choose a Structure:

- Sole proprietor

- Partnership

- S-Corporation

- C-Corporation

- Limited Liability Company (LLC)

- Limited Partnership

Equity Sharing

Insurance

Umbrella Liability

An Attorney's Tale

Darci

Darci Poloni (poloni-law@cox.net) is an attorney in private practice in Henderson, Nevada. She began her career in Los Angeles, California after graduating from the University of Southern California Law School. She moved to Henderson in 2002 and started her law firm, Poloni & Associates, in 2004. Darci focuses her legal practice on estate planning, asset protection and corporate formation and compliance. Darci is passionate about proper planning and enjoys helping her clients avoid probate, leave a legacy for their loved ones, avoid estate taxes to the greatest extent possible and obtain peace of mind. She seeks to help her clients avoid many of the common mistakes that people make due to the improper structuring of their estates and business entities.

> **Darci:** "With regard to corporate formation mistakes, there are lots of examples of companies that were not properly incorporated or formed. If such an entity is subsequently sued, the corporate veil may be pierced thereby exposing the owner's personal assets if a judgment is obtained. Courts may disregard, or 'pierce,' a corporate veil in circumstances where the officers/managers of a company commingle debts and/or expenses with other entities or the owners, the entity is undercapitalized, does not have the appropriate corporate documents in place or the officers/managers do not respect the necessary corporate formalities. I have also seen entities formed as S-Corporations or Limited Liability Companies that elected to be treated for tax purposes as S-Corporations, lose their S-Chapter tax treatment for various reasons resulting in terrible tax ramifications, especially where real property was owned by the corporation."

Darci frequently encounters families and individuals who failed to engage in estate planning and are now dealing with the consequences of their inaction—costly and lengthy probate proceedings. It is not uncommon for the probate process to last two years and cost as much as 9% of a family's assets. Since real estate is generally the most signifi-cant asset that people own, it frequently is affected by the probate pro-cess, resulting in delays of the sale of the family home and/or a reduced sales price. In her practice, Darci tries to help individuals and fami-lies avoid this unfortunate outcome by establishing a living trust and implementing prudent estate planning. Without such planning, there is little that can be done to rectify the situation short of probate.

> **Darci:** "Earlier this year, I was called to a hospi-tal to help a dying mother get her affairs in order. Unfortunately, she died just minutes after I arrived. Obviously, there was no time to ascertain her wishes, prepare her documents or obtain her signature. Her wishes were not honored in the end because her prop-erty passed through probate (it is still pending) and her children will share her property equally. I am told that the mother had intended to leave everything to one daughter who cared for and housed her during her lengthy illness. This situation was very tragic!"

An example of a family that Darci was able to help follows, however, what should be emphasized is that estate planning should occur now rather than when a loved one is facing imminent death.

> **Darci:** "I also recall a tragic story of a couple that meant to do estate planning for years but never got around to it. I got a frantic call on a Thursday eve-ning that the husband would not likely survive the night. I rushed to the hospital, met with the couple to determine what their wishes were, and make sure the husband had his mental faculties. Then rushed back to the office to prepare their living trust and related estate planning documents. Thankfully, we were able

to get all of the documents executed before he passed away, but it was a very difficult time emotionally for both of them. I'm sure they would have rather spent their last precious moments reminiscing rather than taking care of business."

For Darci, the most frustrating part of her practice is dealing with the effects and problems created by people who try to save a little money by doing things themselves or looking for the cheapest solution instead of the one that will achieve the best long-term results.

Darci: "I recently received a call from a gentleman that was trying to do an 'estate planning work-around.' His mother was very ill and gave him financial power of attorney to sell her house before she died. They didn't want to spend $2,000.00 on a trust if she was 'just going to die.' Well, she died before the house sold, thereby voiding the power of attorney, and now the house is stuck in probate in Illinois (her state of residence) and Nevada (the location of the property). Their failure to see the true value of estate planning—her wishes would have been honored in the most cost-effective manner—will now, unfortunately cost them tens of thousands of dollars."

Darci has, literally, dozens of stories like this. The point is to plan properly today to ensure that your ultimate wishes will be followed and that your loved ones will be taken care of in the most efficient manner when you are gone. The tag line for Darci's firm, Poloni & Associates, says it all: *It pays to plan ahead; it wasn't raining when Noah built the ark.*

Chapter 13

Real Estate & Taxes

The hardest thing in the world to understand is the income tax.—**Albert Einstein**

One of the major advantages of owning real estate is the availability of tax benefits. A homeowner is allowed to deduct mortgage interest, points and taxes on a primary residence, as well as a vacation home. In addition, recent changes to the tax code allow for the deduction of PMI, or private mortgage insurance. Of course, there are restrictions as to what is allowed depending on your individual circumstances. The tax laws are constantly changing and it is advisable to consult with a tax professional prior to claiming any deductions.

Investment properties allow for an even greater number of deductions than a personal residence. If you can be considered a *Real Estate Professional,* there is even more available. In addition to *mortgage interest, points* and *taxes,* the owners of investment properties can also deduct the cost of *insurance* on the property, *maintenance* and *repair,* costs associated with obtaining the property, *management fees,* and routine *business expenses,* as well as the costs for *travel and entertainment* related to your real estate business. One of the major deductions is for *depreciation* of the property. Depreciation is a coveted deduction because there are no out-of-pocket expenses associated with it since houses tend to appreciate over time, not depreciate. Other tax benefits can include tax credits for *low-income housing*, and the rehabilitation of *historic properties*. The Internal Revenue Service (IRS) will also have temporary tax incentives available from time to time. One such incentive is the Gulf Opportunity Zone, or *GO Zone*, which was created in the wake of Hurricane Katrina to help with the rebuilding of areas devastated by that 2005 disaster.

The tax code is not just used to collect the money that the government needs to run the country and its ever-growing list of programs and entitlements; it is also a tool that is used to shape the behavior of the taxpayers. Tax deductions and tax credits are used to encourage people to do certain things. The American Dream is home ownership; the government encourages this by allowing taxpayers to deduct certain expenses associated with home ownership from their income, the end result is a smaller income tax bill. These deductions help people to own their home by reducing the amount of their income that is taken from them by the government.

Mortgage Interest

When people buy a home they rarely save the money and then buy the house for cash. They will typically save a lesser amount to be used as a down payment, and then obtain a loan for the balance of the purchase. This loan is called a mortgage and is repaid over a number of years. The lender is paid interest on the amount that is borrowed and this interest can be deducted on the borrower's income tax return. There are limits on the amount of interest that can be deducted. For mortgages obtained after October 13, 1987, the deduction is limited to the interest paid on mortgages of $1,000,000 or less. Interest paid on home equity debt is limited to interest paid on up to $100,000 of debt acquired after October 13, 1987. If you refinance a mortgage, the remaining balance of the original loan is used to determine the amount of interest that is deductible. If you take cash out when you refinance, then you may consider up to $100,000 as debt related to home equity and deduct that.

Example #1	Example # 2
$1,500,000 loan	Refinance
7% interest	Original Loan = $200,000
Annual interest paid = $105,000	New Loan = $350,000
	Interest Rate = 7%
Deductible Amount	Annual Interest = $24,500
$1,000,000 x 7% = $70,000	
	Deductible Amount
	$200,000 + $100,000 Equity
	$300,000 x 7% = $21,000

Points

Points may be deductible as well. A point is actually a form of pre-paid interest. One point is equal to 1% of the loan amount. A mortgage loan of $200,000 that charges 1 point up-front means that you pay $2,000 in points ($200,000 x 1% = $2,000). Points paid on a loan used to acquire a property are fully deductible in the year they were paid. So if you had a mortgage that required you to pay $2,000 in points when you purchased the home, you would be allowed to deduct the amount on your tax return for that year. Points paid on a refinance are not fully deductible in the year paid but must be spread over the life of the loan. So if you paid $2,000 in points when you refinanced, and the loan was for a term of 20 years, you would be able to deduct $100 each year ($2,000/20 = $100). If you were to sell the home, you would be able to deduct the balance remaining in the year the home was sold. One exception to this rule is that you can fully deduct points in the year paid on amounts borrowed for home improvement purposes.

Vacation Homes

Mortgage interest paid on a second home, or vacation home, is also deductible. Points paid to acquire a second home are not fully deductible in the year paid, but must be spread out over the life of the loan. There are rules involving second homes that are rented out for a portion of the year. You must use this home more than 14 days, or more than 10% of the number of days during the year that the home is rented, whichever is longer. If you do not use the home yourself then it will be treated as a rental property. If you do not rent the home out, there is no requirement that you use it at any point during the year.

Real Estate Taxes

Property taxes paid on a primary residence or second home are also deductible in the year paid. Like mortgage interest and points, the amount of real estate taxes paid would be reported on Schedule A of form 1040. Real estate taxes paid on investment properties are fully deductible as well.

Private Mortgage Insurance

One of the more recent additions to the list of deductible items is the deduction for private mortgage insurance, or PMI. PMI is used by lenders when a borrower has less than a 20% down payment. If the borrower defaults on the loan, the insurance will make up a portion the shortfall to the lender in the event that the foreclosure sale does not result in an amount sufficient to pay off the debt. The premium for this insurance is paid by the borrower. Until now this was not a deductible expense. Recent tax law changes allow the borrower to deduct the amount paid for PMI. This deduction applies to mortgages acquired in 2007 and later.

Homeowners generally are not allowed to take deductions for the expenses involved in acquiring a property. Some of these expenses can be added to the basis of the property which could be a benefit if they find them in a position of having to pay capital gains taxes, but other-wise isn't much of a benefit at all.

Investment Properties

When you own investment properties the list of deductible items grows significantly. While you can take the deductions that a home-owner gets, you are also able to take a number of other deductions because you are running a business. Just as typical businesses get to deduct things that are related to running their business, you get to deduct them as well. Just remember that tax laws are constantly chang-ing, what is true today could be different tomorrow.

So what are some of these deductions? For starters, you can deduct many of the costs associated with acquiring the property. Since owning investment properties is a business and the acquisition cost of obtain-ing the property is a cost of doing business, it is usually deductible. Acquisition cost can be found on the HUD-1 form that you receive at closing. These fees can include, but are not limited to, title charges, recording fees, tax stamps, transfer taxes, title insurance and many other items. You can also deduct the cost of home inspections and appraisals. However, you do need to check with a tax professional or the IRS to see what the current law allows.

Insurance

Another deductible item is the cost of insurance for the property. Once again, this is an expense deduction that is not available to a homeowner but is to an investor. If you have insurance on other items related to the property, such as appliances, air conditioning equip-ment, furnaces or any other items, you should be able to deduct those premiums.

Maintenance & Repair

Investment properties will also require routine maintenance and repair. These expenses are a cost of doing business and can be deducted. Maintenance would be the routine things that are required to keep the property in good condition and can include things like landscaping, snow removal, painting and other items of this nature. Repair would be fixing something that has malfunctioned, or broken, such as an air conditioning unit, window, stove, bathroom fixture and so on. A major renovation would not fall into this category, but would be considered a capital improvement. Major improvements would be added to the properties cost basis and deducted through depreciation.

Management & Professional Fees

If you are using the property for rental purposes, you may wish to use the services of a property manager. A property manager will usually charge 8–10% of the gross rent. In turn, they will find and screen tenants, collect rents, handle evictions and arrange for minor repairs as needed. This is also a deductible expense for tax purposes.

A deduction can be taken for professional services. If you retain an attorney to prepare documents and contracts, or to help with other legal items, you can deduct the fees paid. If you hire an accountant or bookkeeper, that cost is also deductible. If you enlist the aid of a consultant to help you in your business, those fees can be written off as well.

Office Expenses

Routine business and office expenses are also deductible. If you rent an office you can write it off. Office supplies, telephone, cell phone, advertising, internet services, Web sites, printing, copies, computer software, ink and toner and just about anything used in the course of business is deductible.

Major investments in your business, such as computer equipment, copiers, furniture and other capital equipment can be depreciated over its' useful life. IRS guides are available outlining the depreciation period for various items. You may choose to take an immediate deduction under section 179 of the tax code instead of depreciating the asset. There are limits as to how much you can deduct in this manner, but it may be a better option depending on your circumstances. Let's assume you were to purchase $10,000 worth of business equipment. You could elect to deduct it all in the current tax year under section 179 or spread the deduction over the useful life of the equipment, which might mean taking a deduction of $2,000 a year for the next five years. Your individual tax situation will determine which method is best for you. This is a case where a consultation with a tax professional is recommended.

Automobile Expenses

Another area open for deduction is your auto expense. Any driving that you do that is related to your business is deductible. You have two choices when it comes to writing off your auto expenses, you can take the IRS allowance for each mile driven for business or you can take a percentage of actual auto expenses. The first step is to determine the percentage of business use for your vehicle. You do this by keeping a diary, or log, of the miles driven. It is a simple habit to develop; you simply record the starting and ending mileage for each business trip that you make. You can add up your business mileage on a weekly or monthly basis and total it all up at the end of the year. You would subtract that mileage from the total mileage driven. You will then have a figure for business miles and personal miles, from which you can figure the percentage of each. Let's assume that you had a 50/50 split of business and personal mileage. You could elect to take a deduction for 50% of all of your auto expenses such as insurance, gas, registration fees, maintenance and a portion of any lease payment or just take the mileage allowance. The mileage allowance is a simpler method, but the percentage of actual expenses may provide a higher deduction. You will need to make that determination based on what is best for you.

Travel & Entertainment

Travel and entertainment is another expense deduction available to you. A word of caution here, this is an area that has been heavily abused and has come under scrutiny by the IRS. The tax code allows you to deduct the cost of any business-related travel. If you travel to look at properties, property you own, or property you are considering buying, the law allows you to deduct your travel expenses such as airfare, lodging and rental car. To qualify the primary purpose of the trip needs to be business related. If you go to Hawaii for a week vacation and look at a vacation condo while you are there, you may wish to think twice about deducting that trip. On the other hand, if you are on vacation and take a cab to go look at potential investment properties, the cab fare would be deductible.

Another frequently abused area is the deduction for business meals. This deduction was so heavily abused that the tax code was changed to allow only 50% of business meals to be deducted. If you are going to deduct meals, you should be sure to keep the receipts and make a note of who you were with and the business that was discussed. If a meal is a legitimate expense you should deduct it, just be sure to keep a record.

Home Office

If you have an office in your home you have the option to deduct it as an expense. Many tax pros recommend that you do not take the deduction if you are located in an appreciating area. If you do choose to take the deduction, you may lose a portion of the capital gains exclusion when you sell the house. If 10% of your home is set aside as an office, then that 10% is not treated as a residence. This means that only 90% of the home will qualify for the capital gains exclusion. Any amount of depreciation could also be subject to recapture (more on that later).

Depreciation

The best deduction may be *depreciation*. The idea behind this is that the value of an asset will erode, or depreciate, over time. This may be true with things like machinery, or equipment, which have a useful life, after which time it needs to be replaced. However, real estate tends to appreciate over time, yet the tax code allows you to write it off as if you are losing value. This is why depreciation is sometimes called a phantom deduction, you have no out-of-pocket expense yet you get a write off as if you do.

The current law allows you to depreciate the value of a residential rental property over a period of 27 years. You are only allowed to depreciate the value of structures, not the land itself. You are allowed a partial deduction in the first year and full deductions until the property is fully depreciated. If you have a property that is worth $320,000, and the land is deemed to be worth $50,000, that means that you can take a depreciation deduction based on the value of the structure, which is

$270,000. A full year of depreciation ($1/27^{th}$) would be $10,000. This deduction makes it possible to legally have a loss in cases where you might otherwise have a profit.

Before you get too excited, there is one drawback and it is called *recapture*. When you eventually sell the investment property you will pay a capital gains tax on the profit. You will also pay a tax on recaptured depreciation. Upon the sale of the house you will total up the amount of depreciation deductions that you have taken. The current tax rate on recaptured depreciation is 25%. Each year the cost basis of the property is reduced by the amount of depreciation that is deducted. This amount is referred to as the *adjusted cost basis*. If the property was sold for an amount that was less the adjusted cost basis, there would be no tax due. If the transaction resulted in a profit, then the recaptured depreciation would be taxed first and then any amount over that would be taxed at the current rate for capital gains, which is now a maximum of 15% for property that is held for more than 1 year.

Temporary Deductions

A temporary change made to the tax code in the area of depreciation involves the government's effort to help restore the areas hit hardest by Hurricane Katrina in 2005. The devastation caused by this natural disaster was tremendous. The government decided that a great way to help the region was to provide incentives to private investors, in order to encourage them to help rebuild the area. This resulted in the creation of the *Gulf Opportunity Zone,* or *GO Zone.* The GO Zone also covers areas hit by Hurricane Rita and Hurricane Wilma.

The GO Zone allows for an additional depreciation deduction of **50%** in the first year. This amount is calculated before the regular deduction is taken. This deduction applies to the areas hit by the storms, which include portions of Florida and Alabama, Mississippi and Louisiana. It is available for non-residential real estate placed into service after August 27, 2005. This temporary incentive is currently slated to end on December 31, 2010. This deduction is not available for a primary residence, only investment property. The property does not need to be new; it just needs to be purchased by you after the effective date. There are many rehab opportunities that meet these criteria.

One major bonus is that the depreciation deduction can be carried back five years to reduce taxes on income that you've already earned. You do this by filing amended tax returns. Depreciation can also be carried forward to future years to offset future income. This is a complicated area of the tax code and consultation with a qualified tax professional is strongly advised.

What does a 50% depreciation deduction really mean? If you purchased a property for $250,000 with a value of $50,000 attributed to the land, you could take a depreciation deduction based on the $200,000 value of the structure. A 50% depreciation deduction means that you could take a $100,000 in the first year! There are limitations on how much of a loss you can show in any given year (currently $25,000), but any unused portion can be carried forward for up to 20 years. If you do not meet the IRS definition of a *Real Estate Professional*, the losses incurred in your real estate investing is considered a passive loss. Passive losses are first used to offset passive income. Any remaining losses can be used to offset ordinary income up to $25,000 as long as your Modified Adjusted Gross Income (MAGI) is not more than $100,000. If your MAGI is more than $100,000, the deduction is phased out at the rate of 50 cents for each additional dollar earned. When your income reaches $150,000, you can no longer take this deduction. Any leftover losses can be carried forward to future years. Using our example of a $100,000 depreciation deduction, and assuming that you had no passive income, you would be able to deduct $25,000 from your income for 4 years or until the remaining depreciation was used up. That is a huge tax incentive.

A *Real Estate Professional* is defined by the IRS as someone who spends a majority of their time in real estate related activities, with more than 750 hours devoted to those activities per year. A real estate professional is not subject to the $25,000 limit because the activity is not considered "passive." Many real estate investors and rehabbers could be considered "professionals" by meeting this IRS test.

In addition to the bonus depreciation, the GO Zone allows for many other incentives including enhanced section 179 deduction, increased tax credit for rehabilitation expenditures, enhanced low income housing credits, tax credits for employers and various tax incentives from state and local governments. With all that is available it would be wise to consult with a professional with knowledge in this area if you wish to take advantage of these opportunities.

Rehabilitation Tax Credit

Another incentive of interest is the *Rehabilitation Tax Credit.* This section of the tax code allows a 10% tax credit for the rehabilitation of *non-historic, non-residential* buildings built before 1936, and a 20% tax credit for the *certified rehabilitation* of *certified historic structures,* which can include residential housing but not the owner's primary residence or vacation property. Rental houses would not qualify, but commercial properties would. To understand what this means you need to understand the difference between a deduction and a credit. A tax deduction allows you to deduct the actual cost of the rehabilitation off of your income; a credit is a dollar-for-dollar reduction in the amount of tax owed. For the sake of simplicity, let's compare a $10,000 tax deduction and a $10,000 tax credit. If you are in the 25% tax bracket, a $10,000 tax deduction will result in a tax savings of $2,500 ($10,000 x 25% = $2,500). A tax credit of $10,000 will reduce the amount of tax owed by $10,000, in this example that would be equivalent to a deduction of $40,000. A Certified Historic Structure is a building that has been certified by the National Parks Service (NPS). The NPS must approve all work that is seeking the 20% credit. There are many requirements and restrictions attached to these credits and the tax laws constantly change so be sure to do your homework if you wish to take advantage of them.

We have covered a lot of ground talking about all of these deductions, but what do they mean? Let's not lose sight of one thing, if you have a deduction that means that you experienced a loss or incurred an expense. If you lose a dollar to a loss or an expense, the IRS allows you to reduce your income by that amount. That does save on the amount of tax owed, but you still lost money. If you are in the 25% tax bracket and lose a dollar, you will save 25 cents in taxes. That means that you still had a net out-of-pocket loss of 75 cents! Losses may seem like a benefit at tax time, but they need to be avoided. Paying taxes just means that you made money and you will not go broke making a profit.

Obviously when you run a business you are going to incur expenses, but you need to keep them manageable. So what do we do with all of these deductions that we have? We use them to offset income. If we are not considered real estate professionals, the income that is earned from real estate is considered "passive," as are the losses. The passive losses are first used to offset passive income. If there are any passive losses remaining, you may be able to use them to reduce your ordinary income. There are rules concerning the deductibility of passive losses, currently you may use them to reduce up to $25,000 if your MAGI is $100,000 or less. The benefit is phased out for higher income taxpayers. Keep in mind that the depreciation deduction may have you showing a loss even though you actually had a positive income.

Example: $150,000 Property

Structure Value = $125,000

Rent = $800/month

Rental Income:	$9,600
Expenses:	(6,000)
Income:	3,600
Depreciation:	(4,630)
Taxable Income:	**(1,030)**

In the example above you had a positive income of $3,600, but because of depreciation you had a taxable loss of $1,030. This is why so many people enjoy investing in real estate, you put money into your pocket, yet you were able to show a loss for tax purposes.

Many rehabbers buy properties with the idea of fixing them and then flipping them for profit, what happens then? To use a classic response, "it depends." When you sell a property you have a capital gain. How that gain is taxed depends on how long you have owned it, and whether it is considered a rental property, an investment property, or a personal residence. If it is a primary residence, and you have lived in it for two out of the last five years, you should qualify for an exclusion from capital gains tax. A single taxpayer is allowed to exclude $250,000 and a married couple, who files a joint tax return, can exclude $500,000 in profit. If the property has not been owned long enough there may be a partial exclusion in certain hardship criteria are met. This is another case where it would be best to seek the advice of a professional.

If it is an investment property you may be taxed as a long-term capital gain, short-term capital gain, or ordinary income. Properties held for less than one year are considered short-term capital gain and are taxed the same as ordinary income. If the property is held for a year or more it could be considered a long-term capital gain and it would qualify for more favorable tax treatment. If there is a large gain in the property the tax savings that you achieve by holding the property long enough to qualify as a long-term gain could be more than the cost of holding the property. You need to do the calculations to see if this is a benefit to you.

Long-term capital gains are taxed at a maximum of 15% currently. If you have a $100,000 gain that qualifies, you would pay a tax of $15,000. If it were taxed as ordinary income and you were in the 25% tax bracket, then you would owe $25,000 in tax. So you pay $10,000 more if you do not qualify for long-term capital gain treatment. If you are close to the long-term point you may wish to consider holding the property, or renting it until it qualifies. You need to look at your situation and see what makes the most sense.

If you are flipping a lot of houses, you may be considered a dealer and you may not qualify for capital gains treatment and may, in fact, be subject to self-employment tax. In this case you should absolutely seek the help of a professional.

1031 Exchange

There is a way to avoid paying the tax now and that is by using a *1031 exchange*. The number "1031" stands for the section of the tax code that it refers to. To quote the IRS, "if you exchange business or investment property solely for business or investment property of a like-kind, no gain or loss is recognized under Internal Revenue Code Section 1031." In this case, like-kind means one investment property is exchanged for another. The properties do not need to be the same, land commercial or single family rentals could be exchanged for an apartment building etc. Of course, there are rules that you have to follow. The primary rule is that you never have access to the money. You also have a limited time frame to complete the exchange. The exchange does not avoid the tax it only delays the payment.

To set up a 1031 exchange you must use a "qualified intermediary" to handle the transaction. When you sell your property the money is sent to a qualified intermediary who will hold it until you close escrow on the new property. After your current property is sold you have 45 days to identify the replacement property and 180 days to complete the transaction. There is no wiggle room when it comes to these dates; if you do not meet the deadline the exchange becomes taxable. You must also use all of the funds from the sale to purchase the replacement property or you will be subject to tax on the amount that is not reinvested. This amount is referred to as "boot."

It is also possible to do a *reverse 1031 exchange*. In a reverse exchange the replacement property is acquired before the property you wish to exchange is sold. When you acquire the new property you have 45 days to identify the property you are going to sell and 180 days to complete the transaction.

The 1031 exchange is a great way to delay paying the capital gain tax but may not be appropriate in all situations. It is something that you should consider when you have a gain in a property you wish to sell. But there are drawbacks, there are fees involved and it works best if you do not need the money from the sale of the existing property. If you are going to do an exchange, be sure to choose carefully when selecting an intermediary. While it is rare, they can fail and you could have trouble retrieving your money if they shut their doors.

Charitable Trust

Another way to avoid the tax on a capital gain is to allow someone to inherit the property. If parents pass property on to their children there is no tax on the capital gain. However the property is included in their estate for the purpose of calculating estate taxes. If the estate is large enough to owe estate taxes then they will need to be paid.

How about if you could avoid the tax altogether? One way to avoid the tax is to give the property away to charity. On the plus side you would get a tax deduction for doing so, on the down side you no longer have the asset. But what if you could give the asset away, earn income from it, get a tax deduction and still pass the value of the asset on to your heirs? It can be done.

A significant estate planning tool allowed by the IRS is the *charitable remainder trust (CRT)*. This is a complicated area of the tax code and needs to be handled by competent attorneys and accountants. The following is a brief, but by no means complete, explanation of how it works.

The first step is to have an attorney who specializes in estate planning, and is familiar with CRTs, to draw up the trust. One or more charities can be named as beneficiaries and a trustee must be selected to administer the trust according to its terms. The trust must be irrevocable, meaning that the terms cannot be changed. The trustee may have the authority to substitute a beneficiary if one should cease to exist.

After the trust is set up it needs to be funded. The person who creates the trust, known as the *grantor*, would then make a gift of the appreciated property to the trust. The trustee can then sell the property and there would be no tax due since the trust is set up for the benefit of a qualified charity. The proceeds of the sale can be invested into other assets, usually income producing securities. A set amount of income is paid to the grantor (current minimum is 5%) who would pay tax on that income.

The grantor also receives a tax deduction for a gift made to charity. This deduction is calculated based on the amount gifted to the trust, age and life expectancy of the grantor(s), and the amount of income being withdrawn. The older the grantor at the time of the gift the greater the deduction will be. The formula is used to calculate the present value of a gift that will be made upon the death of the grantor(s), so the older the grantor is the larger the present value would be.

Sounds good so far, but what about your heirs? If the assets go to charity the heirs would seem to be left out. That isn't necessarily so. The easiest way to take care of that is through life insurance. As long as at least one of the grantors is qualified to purchase life insurance then the assets can be replaced. A life insurance policy could cost significantly less than the tax savings. If there is an estate tax issue it may be necessary to create a life insurance trust to own the policy so that it is kept outside of the grantors' estate. The attorney can determine the best way to proceed in this regard.

Going the route of a CRT would generally be done only in the case of a significant tax situation. It can be costly to set up and it involves the participation of several professionals such as accountants, attorneys, insurance agents and investment professionals. Most people would not go through this trouble but for some it may be well worth it.

Summary

Homeowner Deductions:

- Mortgage Interest
- Real Estate Taxes
- Points
- Private Mortgage Insurance (PMI)

Investor Deductions:

- Mortgage Interest
- Real Estate Taxes
- Points
- Depreciation
- Insurance
- Maintenance & Repair
- Management & Professional Fees
- Automobile Expenses
- Travel & Entertainment
- Office Expenses

An Accountant's Tale

Judy

Judy Cruden (jrccpa@cox.net) is a Certified Public Accountant (CPA) in Las Vegas, Nevada. She graduated from UNLV and began her accounting career 16 years ago and has been in private practice for the past ten. She is a real estate investor herself and her firm, Judith Cruden, CPA has a large number of real estate investors as clients. Her experience with her own investments gives her a unique perspective when it comes to tax matters involving real estate.

One of the things that frustrate her is that people do not plan ahead when it comes to taxes. When someone is having their taxes prepared in April it is too late to change something that they did in the previous year. This is particularly frequent with regards to new investors.

> **Judy:** "The most common investing mistake I come across is new investors, (sometimes seasoned ones as well), not understanding that when you sell a property and you didn't utilize a 1031 exchange, there are capital gains to pay AND that investing the proceeds into another real estate project DOES NOT reduce the capital gain. Nor is the down payment deductible as an expense. The other common mistake is not keeping good records when you have an investment."

Judy has also come across situations where people thought that they knew what they were doing only to find out that they had it all wrong. In some situations correcting the error is a simple matter but in others it can be a complete disaster.

> **Judy:** "I had a new client come to me who was a realtor for 5+ years. This realtor came into some money of his own and decided to become an investor himself. During the course of the year he purchased a total of

seven residential investment properties. He rehabbed and then sold four of those properties in the same year. The short-term capital gains on those four flips were a total of $220,000. He then used those proceeds (not through a 1031 Exchange) to purchase the additional three properties that he planned to hold & rent. He used all the funds as down payments so that he had low monthly payments & positive cash flow monthly from the rentals he was holding. What he didn't know was that he couldn't deduct the $220,000 of down payments he had done, nor could he defer any of the gain on the four properties sold. There was nothing that could be done as he had come to me AFTER the transactions had taken place. He owed taxes on a short-term capital gain of $72,600 and had no cash to pay the tax bill. Since short-term capital gains are taxed at ordinary income rates, he also didn't get to utilize the 15% long-term capital gain rates.

With proper tax planning, the tax bill could have been much less. He now calls me before he does any transaction to be sure it has been structured properly."

Unfortunately horror stories, such as these, are all too common. Many people are reluctant to consult with tax professionals because they fear the cost. Other people figure that they could just as easily do it themselves. While a W-2 employee with a limited amount of deductions can probably prepare his own tax return with little difficulty, the intricacies of real estate investing are another matter altogether. The impact of taxation can have a great effect on many real estate transactions.

Judy: "Everything in real estate taxation is determined by the intent of the parties, the holding periods and the type of transaction. It is always better to plan rather than try to do damage control after the fact."

Unfortunately many people do not come to realize the value of professional advice until they do something wrong and experience a financial loss. The old adage shown on a TV commercial that says "you can pay me now, or you can pay me later" is so true. There are so many tax advantages available to real estate investors but you can't take advantage of them if you don't know about them. As far as the IRS is concerned "I didn't know" is not an acceptable excuse. Using a seasoned tax professional such as Judy can pay huge dividends in the long run.

Chapter 14

Resources

If opportunity doesn't knock, build a door.
—Milton Berle

The key to getting started is to get educated. Take the time to learn as much about the business as you can. Experience is definitely the best teacher, and you will learn more from doing your first project than any book or seminar can teach you. That doesn't mean that you should just dive in and learn as you go. There are many different ways to get educated and you should use as many different methods as possible. Some of these resources are free, some cost a little, while others can be quite expensive.

Books & Tapes

There are many books and tapes available on various aspects of real estate investing. Some of these may be available at your local library. That is a great place to start since it is free. If you do not have any real estate investing experience, you should start with the basics and work your way up from there. There are many different books on rehabbing, be sure to find ones that tell the real story, not ones that just hype how rich you are going to be. You can also find plenty of books and tapes at traditional bookstores as well as online retailers. Online auction sites are also a great place to find books, tapes and courses that are being resold. When looking at any of these items you need to be sure to see how current the information is. Some information and concepts will never be outdated but other things, like the tax information, may have changed considerably.

There are some books that are about investing in general that can have a lot to do with investing in real estate. Other books will deal with your mindset and help you look at things in a different light. One book that comes to mind is *Think and Grow Rich*, by Napoleon Hill. This book was originally written in 1937, but it is just as valid today. It shows how positive thinking can have a profound impact on your life.

A more recent work that is extremely popular is *Rich Dad, Poor Dad*, by Robert Kiyosaki. This book challenges you to reevaluate the way you think about things. It attempts to explain how the rich think differently than the poor when it comes to money. Real estate is a very heavy theme in this book, but it applies to all matters in regards to money.

One book that I find to be extremely enlightening is *Extraordinary Popular Delusions & Madness of Crowds*, by Charles Mackay. It explores crowd psychology and investment manias through history. It shows how people ignore logic and reason and get caught up in the hysteria of an investment fad. The amazing thing is that this book was first published in 1841! History does repeat itself, and the lessons in this book are just as valid today as they were when it was written. Investment booms that led to bubbles that burst are not aberrations, but a normal part of our economy. Learning about the past manias can help you to recognize when it happens today.

There are many books that can be highly inspirational and impact your business. You may wish to read *The Millionaire Next Door: The surprising Secrets of America's Wealthy*, by Thomas J. Stanley, which explores how the wealthy live their lives. Another classic is *The Richest Man in Babylon*, by George S. Clason, originally written in 1926, the common sense wisdom in the book is timeless. Another book that directly pertains to real estate investing is *The Weekend Millionaire's Secrets to Investing in Real Estate* by Mike Summey and Roger Dawson. This book explains how to become wealthy in your spare time.

All of these books have a lot to share, but there is no real "secret." The simple truth is that you need to work hard and follow a program that suits you. The books can provide knowledge and inspiration, but you still need to do the work. Many people will read books such as these yet never act on them, those who do can become fabulously wealthy.

Seminars

There may be free seminars available in your area. Just as there is no "free lunch," these seminars aren't really free. They are put on by a company or individual that is looking to sell something. That doesn't mean that there is no value or that you cannot learn from it. When attending one of these "freebies," you need to look at the underlying motivation of the sponsor, what are they trying to sell? Do not take the information at face value and remember that there is no "best" or "only" way to do something. Seminars may be put on by mortgage companies or brokers, banks, real estate firms, insurance companies and others looking for new business. By hosting a seminar these companies hope to show you that they are knowledgeable and would be a good firm to deal with, many of them are. But beware of firms that are just trying to make a fast buck by pushing something that may not be appropriate.

Many so-called "gurus" will take out large newspaper ads touting a free seminar that is held at a major hotel or conference center. The primary purpose of these seminars is to sell you their programs, books, tapes, courses, boot camps and mentoring programs. These programs can run from a few hundred dollars to tens of thousands of dollars. They may be of value to some people, but for others it winds up being a very poor investment. If you attend one of these seminars do so with your eyes open and be sure that you are getting something that will be useful to you if you do invest in a program.

Boot Camps

There are many investment "gurus" out there who claim that they are successful real estate investors and that they can teach you to be too. Some of them have legitimately earned millions investing in real estate, while others are outright frauds. The vast majority seem to fall somewhere in the middle. They may have had some investment success, but find that they can make a lot more money telling others how to do it. Remember the old adage, "Those who can, do. Those who can't, teach."

One distinction to look for is whether they are talking about real estate in general, or are they talking about your specific market. A program that is tailored to your market will probably have a much greater impact on your business than one that is general in nature. If the program targets a specific investment strategy you will probably find a greater benefit than one that takes a shotgun approach and gives you little tidbits of many different techniques.

Unfortunately, the goal of many of these boot camps is not to teach you how to invest in real estate, but to show you how much more you have to learn. After spending several thousand dollars and two or three intense days, they try to convince you that you need to work with them to be successful. Of course, the way to do that is by spending thousands of dollars on their mentoring program or advanced courses.

Mentoring Programs

One type of program to be especially wary of is a *mentoring program*. Any mentoring program is only as good as the person that you are hiring to mentor you. If you are considering a mentor, it should be one who has already achieved what you are looking to accomplish. If you want to be successful at rehabs, it makes little sense to work with a mentor who specializes in apartment buildings. Does this mentor have the credentials that he claims? Has the mentor had success in down markets as well as up markets? It doesn't take a genius to make money when markets are booming, but it does take skill to find profitable deals in a poor market. There are plenty of people who will be happy to take your money, be sure that you get what you pay for.

There are many horror stories of people who didn't do their homework and were burned because they trusted a mentor. I know of one such couple who attended a seminar, which led to a boot camp. After spending several thousand to attend the weekend workshops, they decided that to be successful they would need to sign up for the mentoring program. They paid a total that was in excess of $20,000, but they were assured that they would make that back in one deal. They were looking to invest in the high-flying Las Vegas market because they felt the boom was only going to continue. Their so-called mentor coached them through the purchase of a house at full retail, which they then rented out. They were left with a negative cash flow that was greater than $500 per month. They were told not to worry about the negative outlay because they were going to make so much more through appreciation. The sad end to the story is that the Las Vegas market peaked and they were stuck with a house they couldn't afford. The final result was that they couldn't get rid of the house and they lost it to foreclosure. They also lost their down payment, the two years of negative cash flow and had nothing to show for the more than $20,000 they paid to learn how to do this. Their total loss was in excess of $100,000. To make matters worse, the money had come from an equity loan on their primary residence.

Are all mentoring programs bad? Absolutely not, you just need to go in with your eyes wide open. Be sure that the mentor knows what they are doing and that you have a clear understanding as to what you can expect.

Real Estate Investment Clubs

If you are serious about real estate investing you should join a *real estate investment club*. These clubs are located throughout the country. Some are part of a large network of clubs, while others may be a group of local investors who meet informally. These meetings will usually feature an educational topic about some aspect of real estate investing. You have the opportunity to "mix and mingle" with other investors. You will also people who are involved in various aspects of real estate investing such as mortgage brokers, real estate agents, escrow officers, appraisers and many other professionals in related industries. You may also be offered various investment opportunities in which you can participate. If considering investing in one of these opportunities, you need to investigate it just as you would any other real estate deal and not fall for a slick sales pitch. Clubs will frequently have sponsors for the meetings to help defray the cost of the event. The sponsor will usually get an opportunity to share their product or service in a brief presentation to the group.

If you are debating about joining a club, be sure to see if the club has a specific agenda. Some clubs are formed by real estate firms or mortgage brokers who are just looking to get your business. You should seek out clubs that are truly designed as a way for investors to come together and share ideas and information.

Networking Groups

Networking groups are a great way to get the word out about what you are doing. These groups are made up of business people who meet, over breakfast or lunch, on a regular basis. The primary purpose of the group is to exchange information and leads in order to help the members grow their business. Like the real estate clubs, some networking groups are a part of a large network of clubs, while others are much less formal. The idea is to get the word out about what you are looking for. The person that you are speaking to may not have a run-down house to sell you, but he may know someone who does. That is the essence of networking. If you join a networking group you must be prepared to give as well as receive. Just as you are looking for others to help you in your business, you should be prepared to try to help them as well.

Service organizations are another form of networking group. These clubs, such as Rotary International, Lions, Kiwanis, Elks, and Knights of Columbus, exist in almost every town. Their main focus is to serve the people of the community, but it is also a great place to develop relationships with other business people in the community.

Associations

Another way to network with others is through trade or business associations. You may wish to join the local Chamber of Commerce, which is made up of local business owners. Many chambers have mixers, educational seminars and other events that you can attend. Some of these events are for members only, while others will be open to the public. If you are employed in a real estate related field you may wish to join a trade association. Realtors, lenders, appraisers, home inspectors, escrow officers and others have industry associations that you can join for the purpose of continuing education as well as networking with others in your field. These associations are a great way to stay abreast of what is happening in your real estate market.

Web Sites

There are many useful Web sites that have something to do with real estate. It may be a government Web site such as EPA.gov that deals with environmental issues, or Homesales.gov, which deals with government owned homes, or it could be a number of different organizations. The National Association of Home Inspectors, at Nahi.org, or the American Society of Home Inspectors, at Ashi.org, represents home inspectors. Real estate agents have Realtor.com as a resource, and there are plenty of other Web sites to visit. Use a search engine to find what you are looking for.

There are on-line networking communities where investors meet to share information. *Wanna Network* (wannanetwork.com) is a community with over 12,000 members, which include real estate agents, mortgage professionals, escrow officers, and investors who get together for the purpose of keeping up with real estate trends throughout the country.

Another site is *Bigger Pockets* (biggerpockets.com), with well over 13,000 members and growing. This site is geared more towards investors, although you will also find agents and lenders as well. The site has very strict rules on soliciting which keeps away the spammers. The forum section is very welcoming to novice investors and veterans alike. They also regularly post articles on various real estate topics and have numerous tools and resources available through the site.

For those who are interested in investing in other markets, you have the National Association of Residential Real Estate Investment Advisors (Narreia.com). This site screens their advisors to be sure that they have the knowledge and experience required in order to deal with investors. The advisors are located across the country and contribute articles regularly, which allow investors to keep informed of what is happening in other parts of the United States. The site is also loaded with various investment articles and useful tools to help you with investment decisions.

The best thing about the sites above is that they are free of charge. There is a wealth of information that you might otherwise pay a substantial fee to acquire.

People

Your best resource is people. Everyone knows somebody who knows someone who needs something. It is all about making connections and developing relationships with as many people as possible. You should have your business cards with you wherever you go. You never know where your next deal is going to come from or who you might meet that could help you. So the bottom line is that you should always be prepared. Make sure that everyone knows what you do and what you are looking for.

Summary

Resources:

- Books & Tapes

- Seminars

- Boot Camps

- Mentoring Programs

- Real Estate Investment Clubs

- Networking Groups

- Associations

- Web Sites

- People

A Rehabber's Tale
Bell Avenue

The summer of 2007 saw a great number of changes in the world of real estate investing. Once red-hot markets had come screeching to a halt, interest rates on adjustable rate loans were ratcheting up and homeowners were unable to refinance to lower their payments. Foreclosures were occurring at unprecedented rates because people were unable to make the new higher payments or sell the houses that were now, in many cases, worth significantly less than the balance on the mortgage. This seemed like a great opportunity to find bargains among the many desperate sellers, or from the banks that now owned homes that they had foreclosed on.

One of my friends had located just such a bank-owned property and had asked me to partner with her on the rehab. The numbers worked and, while it needed rehab, it was in good enough condition to qualify for conventional financing. We would be able to complete a fast rehab and list it for price that was far enough below market to attract a buyer quickly. The financing had been approved and a contractor was prepared to start working as soon as we closed escrow.

At this point, just prior to close of escrow, the wheels fell off. The financing had been arranged through a lender that dealt primarily with investor loans. They received their funding through American Home Mortgage, which was one of the largest companies of its kind. The meltdown of the sub-prime lending companies had created a ripple effect that led to American Home Mortgage declaring bankruptcy. So much for our loan commitment, there was no money available to lend.

We located another lender who would be able to do the deal and proceeded in that direction. Prior to closing, however, the lender said that they would need a much larger down payment and that the terms would not be as good as they had initially quoted. This, plus the fact that the market was spiraling downward, caused us to cancel the purchase. As the weeks passed we were happy that we had let the deal die.

In a classic example of one door closing and another opening, I received a phone call from one of my real estate agents. It seems that a hot deal was available in Ely, Nevada. There was a three-bedroom house in a good part of town that was being sold by an estate. Even though it needed a lot of work, it was listed well below what it should sell for. Of course, this got my attention. The perception that the market was soft, plus the fact that it needed to be an as-is, all-cash purchase, had scared away potential buyers.

I looked at the property and found that it had been built in 1940, but had not had any significant upgrades. It needed a new kitchen, bathroom, electrical upgrade, roof and landscaping work, as well as paint and new carpets. On the plus side, it had a fairly new water heater and the furnace was in excellent condition. Closer inspection found that the insulation in the attic was inadequate and the walls had no insulation at all. And this was a town the routinely experienced sub-zero temperatures in winter!

I estimated that the work would cost about $25,000 and I added a cushion of $5,000 for the inevitable surprises. The house would be worth about $150,000 after renovations, and that was a conservative estimate. Why my agent thought this was a good deal was the fact that they were only asking $65,000. This truly was a hot deal and I gladly would have paid the asking price. However, I knew that the as-is, all-cash terms would eliminate many buyers and the house had not yet received any offers.

I had my agent submit an offer of $48,000, which was 25% below the asking price and only about 33% of the value after repair. I was expecting either an outright rejection, or a counter offer that was closer to the asking price. Much to my surprise, and delight, the offer was accepted as written. Little did I know that the fun was just beginning.

This was an estate sale that needed to be approved by the court. In Nevada, this required that a public notice be placed in the local newspaper for three consecutive weeks, listing the date and time of the court proceeding. I also learned that anyone could show up at the hearing and place a bid, as long as it was 5% higher than mine. If that happened, I would have the option of bidding again. This would continue until only one bidder remained. There was no way of knowing in advance if there would be other bidders. I fully expected that the legal notice would result in competition and I was prepared to increase my bid. Much to my relief, I was the only one there and the court approved the sale.

This entire process had taken in excess of three months and it was now the dead of winter. The work on the exterior was going to have to wait. I'm not upset about that since this will be a fairly long project and there is plenty of work to be done on the inside. The early stage of the demolition has not resulted in any unexpected problems. Other than the lack of insulation I am very impressed with the overall quality of the materials used and the construction techniques that were employed in 1940. It seems that they didn't try to cut corners back then, and quality was highly valued.

I am very excited about this project and the potential of the house. While it is just getting started, I can picture the end result.

And the tale continues....

Chapter 15

Final Thoughts

Success seems to be connected with action.
Successful people keep moving. They make mistakes,
but they don't quit.—**Conrad Hilton, Hotel Executive**

By now you've absorbed a lot of information. If you have figured nothing else out, remember this: rehabbing works in any market. When you purchase a property to rehab, you make your money going in by purchasing at a discount. In a market where houses aren't selling well you just need to pay a lot less to make the deal profitable. If you pay too much, you will lose most of the time.

Rehabbing will also make you popular with the neighbors. The people who live around a house being rehabbed benefit almost as much as the rehabber does. When the eyesore of the block becomes a nice house, the values of adjacent properties are no longer being dragged down. When I'm working on a rehab project it is quite common for the neighbors to come around to see what I'm doing. They are invariably happy to see me.

Renovating houses also serves as a creative outlet. You get to use your imagination when planning your project and creating your masterpiece.

You get to sharpen your problem solving skills because you will always be running into problems. When a house has been finished, you will have a real sense of accomplishment. Even if the project doesn't turn out exactly like you expected you will still have done something amazing.

Before you jump into the business be sure that you have laid the groundwork. When a skyscraper is built they spend a lot of time digging down deep to build a strong foundation. Take care of putting your personal finances in order. Create a budget and be sure to have sufficient reserves before you start. Develop additional streams of income, even a little bit extra can be a big help when things are tight.

Set goals for your business and set personal goals as well. Your odds of success will be so much greater if you have an end result in mind. Create a dream board to help you visualize those goals. It may seem strange if you've never done it, but it will become addictive when you see that it works. That dream board will be a daily reminder of what you hope to accomplish and it will help you stay on track.

You should have a plan and work your plan. Whether it is a formal, well-designed business plan or just something that you scratched out on a napkin, you need to follow it. If you are jumping all over the place it will be very hard to succeed. You should also select the appropriate structure for your business. The structure can evolve as your business grows. You may start as a sole proprietorship and later become an LLC or a corporation.

Think carefully about what type of rehab project you are looking to do as your first one. Rehabbing a house for personal use is how a great many rehabbers began their business. The process itself can be intoxicating. Once you have completed a project you can't wait to do another. Rehabbing for personal use has a much lower level of risk than rehabbing to flip or rent. If the project takes longer than expected it doesn't matter as much. If it cost more than you thought you can slow the project down until you have the money.

The hardest, and often most frustrating, part of the business is actually finding a suitable property. Remember that you should not take shortcuts. Do your homework and do the proper legwork. If you are doing it right you should be walking away from most of the deals that you see. You are looking for that one true diamond in the rough. There are many run down houses, but that doesn't mean that you can make money on them. You should be out looking at houses as much as possible. You need to work your farm and work your network. If you do that enough, you will come to know when you have a good deal.

Be sure to evaluate any potential deal and evaluate your own ability to do the project. One of the easiest ways to lose money is to get in over your head. Your first project should be relatively small. You can work your way up to bigger and bigger projects as you gain experience. One of the most important items to remember is that you need to "know what you don't know." If you don't know something, then you have to find someone who does.

If you are going to make your money when you buy, then you need to be sure to buy at the right price. Always keep the winning formula in mind:

$$(ARV \times 70\%) - Repairs = Maximum \ Price$$

Make your offers with that maximum price in mind. Of course, you always want to do better if you can. Learn to negotiate well, if you don't get your price you should move on. Be sure you don't fall into the trap of becoming emotionally involved with the house; if you do you'll wind up paying too much.

Financing is a huge part of any deal. It can easily add 10–15% to the total cost. If you have a poor financing arrangement it can be very difficult to turn a profit. Work with a lender that you can respect and trust, someone who really knows the business. The last thing you want is to do a tremendous amount of work that result in everyone making money but you.

Managing the project is incredibly important. You need to stay on top of all aspects of the job. Just because you are working with a contractor doesn't mean that you can sit back and relax. The TV programs are always showing people who get lazy and allow the contractors to mess up. Your primary responsibility is to manage the project from beginning to end. That means that you need to be there as often as humanly possible. Guaranteed if you take time off to do other things, something will go wrong.

When selling the property be sure to price it right. Every day the house sits is costing you money and eating away at your profit. If you price it too aggressively the house will sit on the market for a long time. No matter what the market conditions, it should be priced at a point that will result in a sale in 30 days or less. If you aren't getting any offers then you've priced it too high. Avoid the temptation to get greedy, if you get an offer that is reasonable you should make the deal happen and go on to the next one. You won't go broke making a profit.

Once again be sure to watch your emotions. After you've put a lot of blood sweat and tears into a project it is only natural to get attached to it. Don't take it personally if someone doesn't appreciate your masterpiece, we all have different needs, desires and tastes. What you think is exceptional someone else may see as ordinary.

Always remember that you have a partner in every deal, Uncle Sam. He is going to want his cut. Keep taxes in mind throughout the process and consult with your accountant. Proper planning could save you a lot of money. The timing of a deal could have a lot to do with how much you pay and when you pay it.

Be sure to use all of the resources available to you. Real estate clubs, networking groups and other associations can be a great help. Take advantage of courses, books, tapes, seminars and Web sites. Just be sure that if you are paying for it, that you are getting something of value in return.

One of your greatest resources is learning from people who have "been there, done that." It's one thing to learn from your own mistakes, but it's usually a lot less expensive to learn from the mistakes of others. Most people are very willing to share their experiences, let them and learn from them.

Avoid being too optimistic. It is normal for you to take all of this information and want to jump on a deal immediately. That feeling is called *"gotta-do-a-deal-it is,"* avoid that temptation! Don't do a deal for the sake of doing a deal, make sure the numbers work.

Numbers don't lie, a deal either works or it doesn't. In the end the results will show in your bank account, you either made money or you lost it. Manipulating the numbers to make you feel better about a transaction doesn't make the end result any different. You can fool yourself, but you can't trick the deal.

The Rehabber's Eye

As you gain experience you will be amazed at how your vision changes. You will look at that pitiful piece of real estate and envision what it will look like when it is finished. You will see past the peeling paint, worn out roof and overgrown yard. Instead you will see a beautiful home with great landscaping and outstanding curb appeal. That vision gets better and better with each completed project. Eventually it seems that you can plan the entire project in your head. When that happens you have acquired the *rehabber's eye*, use it wisely.

Happy Rehabbing!

Be sure to visit www.RehabersEye.com

978-0-595-48631-1
0-595-48631-2

Printed in the United States
108199LV00001B/102/P

9 780595 486311